SING *YOUR* SONG

HOW TO SILENCE DOUBT AND USE YOUR GOD-GIVEN TALENTS

NADINE A. BLAIR

ISBN: Paperback: 978-976-96462-0-9
            Kindle: 978-976-96462-1-6

Table of Contents

Acknowledgements v

Foreword..7

INTRODUCTION...9

Chapter 1: SING YOUR SONG – The Birthing 13

Chapter 2: SING YOUR SONG – While You Wait 29

Chapter 3: SING YOUR SONG – Even When Life Gets Bitter.........41

Chapter 4: SING YOUR SONG – Break the Chains with Your Praise!
....53

Chapter 5: SING YOUR SONG – Trust His Heart; Follow His Lead ..69

Chapter 6: SING YOUR SONG – Happiness is a State of Mind 79

Chapter 7: SING YOUR SONG – When There Is Nothing Else You
Can Do – Literally! 89

Chapter 8: SING YOUR SONG – And Change the World 95

Chapter 9: SING YOUR SONG – You Were Made for This!...........101

Chapter 10: SING YOUR SONG – Singing Life Through A Valley of
Death...117

Chapter 11: SING YOUR SONG – What's the Worst That Could
Happen?..129

About The Author 139

Acknowledgements

For all the times You my Heavenly Father have waited patiently for me to simply get it – that you love me and you Favour me…THANK YOU!

My Abba Father – Jehovah God – All praise and Glory belong to You. Thank you for giving me one more chance.

My Sweet Jesus – The Christ – The Son of the Living God – I thank You. All the Honour – All the Glory and All the Praise be to You.

Thanks to my family. My Father, Bishop Dr. Ronald Blair, for your deep devotional gift of sharing the word; my mother, Rev. Evon Blair, for your spark of life and energy. I got it from you. Thank you mom for the pleasant surprise and for following the leading of the Holy Spirit and writing my Foreword.

My sisters who keep me in check – Delva and her family – you mean the world to me sis. Please just record one song for me – one; Novia who has it all together – well you look like it and I admire you; Paula you are full of talent girl and your calm spirit is encouraging and my niece, Ruthann, who pushes me to be better (she literally just came and said to me "Auntie when you gonna finish your book" – told yah!).

To Author Marsha A Malcolm whom I have never met in person but who I am so grateful to have met and talked with on the phone. First of all – buy her books – look them up – she is an excellent writer; secondly Marsha – the coffee is coming – lol. Thank you Marsha – I am forever grateful – for all the help with getting my book to this stage.

Tevaun Brown – who during a message one day just turned around under the leading of the Holy Spirit and told me there is a book in me…wow. Thank you for being obedient.

Ava-Gay Blair – You are truly a wonderful encouragement to me. I love you sis. I pray you all the best – and your book…books – what a blessing! Keep writing sis. Thank you.

To Drs. Derek and Dorette Senior, thank you for allowing your home and conference to be the "operation room" for the birth of the song that led to this book. Thank you for your continued support of the worship ministry.

To C. Orville McLeish, author, publisher, playwright and more – thank you for your guidance and assistance. I wanna be like you when I get a little older. So proud of you. (He has written so many books and plays – now this is a story worth sharing).

Perpetual Sounds of Praise team – From the year 2002 until now – every single singer, musician and worker who played a part…I could not have done it without you. Look out for the Book of Honours coming out…I have to say thank you…again.

Fans – all my fans from the Love 101 FM family. You give me the energy to get to work – even in a pandemic. I want to be there for you – to encourage and uplift you with a word or song. You mean so much to me. Thank you.

I want to specially acknowledge those who contributed to the front page design: Artwork done by Toni-Kay Bromfield and the Involve Media Team; Makeup by Lyric Rochester, Makeup Artist and Business Mogul (Instagram @LyricRochester); Outfit by FHL Designs (Faith Hope Love) Instagram @ fhldesignsja. The back page was designed by C. Orville McLeish; Outfit by Heather Laine (Instagram @ heatherlaineclothing).

Foreword

It has taken a long time to come, but finally it is here! As her mother, I can say emphatically, I am glad it did not come before. This is God's timing and God's timing is always right.

It has not been an easy road for the writer. I have watched her go through some of the hardest seasons of life. There were times of immense fear, timidity, pain, hurt, failure, criticism, rejection, and so many "tragic" experiences that have left many scars. But guess what, I have seen her cry her way through; weep her way through; confess her way through; pray her way through; worship her way through until she got the release to "sing her song" from a clean, pure, grateful and loving heart.

So why do people sing songs? People sing songs, just for 'singing songs'. People sing songs because of the 'beat' of the song. Others sing songs because of the lyrics. Yet others sing songs because of the message it brings to them. Still others 'sing songs' which are birthed through life's experiences.

Moses and the children of Israel had a nerve-wracking experience facing the Red Sea, with mountains on either sides and the enemy pursuing them. God gave them instructions how to cross over. Stretch that rod in your hand over the "uncrossable waters", God told him. He did. The rest is history. The children of Israel crossed the Red Sea on dry land.

And what was their response to this miracle? Led by Moses, they began to "sing their song" birthed out of that frightening experience, when God came through for them.

Who is like unto thee, O LORD, among the gods? who is like thee, glorious in holiness, fearful in praises, doing wonders?
Exodus 15:11 KJV

This writer can justly write this book SING YOUR SONG, because it is birthed through her life's grilling experiences.

No one has to stay on the bad and difficult side of your problems. Not at all. You don't have to live in defeat all the days of your life. Rise up and 'sing your song'. Sing a new song. Sing a song of victory.

May you find hope, life, peace and favour with God as you read these Holy Ghost directed pages and learn to give praise and honour to God who has dealt wondrously with you.

Rev. Evon Blair
Retired Minister of the New Testament Church of God, Jamaica
Served with her husband, Bishop Dr Ronald Blair
Mother of Nadine A Blair

Introduction

Welcome to a journey about my struggle as a writer. A struggle to believe that I was "good enough" or had what it takes to write. A journey that continues two books down and more in me to come.

It took me years to start writing books. And then years again to finish. My first book, at the time of writing *this* book, is still unfinished. So, this is actually my second book that will be published first. My 53rd birthday was coming up and I just knew I needed to do something. In the past I had done worship events, A Night of Honour – recognizing some persons who had contributed to my life and ministry and I had also done a banquet and praise night on my 50th birthday.

I felt like something was missing. I had done all these things in the past few years and braps – I would be 53 and nothing.

And just like that, all I could hear in my spirit was SING YOUR SONG! Sing Your Song? Write a book on the journey of song writing and the lessons learnt.

It was loud. It was clear.

That was my cue. This is the fruit.

This writing journey was hard. I had to drown out the many voices in my head telling me not to bother to write. I had to be strong and just get on with it. My prayer, my dream is that you will receive what I believe is a now word for every single one of us. Don't wait. Just go! You are good enough because God made you great. You are strong enough because when you lose strength, once you cry out to Him – His strength is perfect.

God is interested in every concern – the big ones and the little ones. And He made each of us with a unique gift and ability. We may all do one thing but how it is done will be different. That's just God.

Sing Your Song is a bidding to go where you have not gone before; a call to do your own thing – that God-assigned task that has been waiting to be birthed.

Each chapter will take you on a journey of songs and poems the Lord has given me and songs I have come to love over the years. My prayer is that the stories behind each song will bless you.

You may not write songs or poems but we all struggle at some point to believe.

What if we took Proverbs 23:7 to heart – *"For as he thinks in his heart, so is he."* NKJV

I believe that if you can think it – so it is! I woke up one morning with the urge to pray against procrastination. Why do we wait on the perfect time? The perfect comments from people... The perfect this or the perfect that. We have the One True Living God who gives us the perfect steps to being all we can be.

Sing Your Song!

Get up from your mundane dance of the norm.
Step to the rhythm of your Almighty God
Face each adversity, trial and storm.
God has already overcome
All you will face on this trod.

Written by Nadine Blair
NADSINK
November 16, 2019

I write poems. Always have. As you read, you will notice that each chapter has poems. That is a gift by the Holy Spirit. One I give Him all the credit for.

I love the poetry style that accommodates a rhyme and rhythm. Others like prose and thoughtful flow without the rhyme. My point? Whatever you like – poems, prose, songs or other – and whatever the format you like – Do it! Get up! Get Going! And SING YOUR SONG.

I also believe with all my heart that the Lord loves to hear when we sing to Him. Even if it is off-key – but let those be in your quiet times... OK?! Smile! From your heart sing a new song unto the Lord. And let it flow from a heart of genuine praise and adoration unto your God.

Sing and make melody to the Lord. Desire nothing more than to be in His presence and to please Him daily. Let your life be that of a song – a life symphony to the King of all kings and the Lord of all lords. I trust this book will inspire you to:

Be the best you, you can be
Give your best to the Master first and
Share your best with your world

Start or continue that business idea, book, even a movie – whatever it is. Let faith arise in your soul – take wings and fly and SING YOUR SONG.

Selah.

Chapter 1
SING YOUR SONG - The Birthing

It was November 2015 and Drs Senior had invited Perpetual Praise to be guests at their Conference in Connecticut. Myself, singer Kerina and keyboardist Brinton boarded our flight and took the trip to cold, cold Connecticut to the home of Drs Derek and Dorrett Senior en route to a lovely getaway location for their annual conference. It was important for us to rehearse and prepare for the conference. We were settled in the living room and we were just singing and worshipping and enjoying Jesus... and then just like that, it began to flow.

Verse 1
There are times when life gets so confusing,
What shall I do, just where do I begin?
But there's a place where I can find assurance,
His Word reminds me this is not the end.
So I get away into my quiet place
And there I bask in His mercy and His grace
And I say to Him

Chorus
Way Maker
Joy Giver
Peace Speaker
That's Who You are to me

My Healer
Strong Tower
Redeemer
That's Who You are to me.

It came easily. The words flowed from my mouth and from pen to paper they were inked into being. Brinton played and I truly believe it was a God-moment. It is in these times that I am amazed at how God can just pour a thought into our minds and we respond with a song... His gifting knows no bounds.

The words were easy because in them lie:

- ∂ the secret prescription for every aching pain
- ∂ the panacea that every doctor wants to put their hand on
- ∂ the answer for every possible question
- ∂ the remedy for every broken heart, puzzled mind and disappointed soul

In HIS presence there is not just fullness of joy – but peace abounding and direction. And so, as the Holy Spirit continued to pour out His blessing, I continued to write as Brinton played...

Verse 2
I'm sure to grow when I am in Your presence
My will gets lost in Yours and I'm at peace
And no matter what I face I know the outcome
Is for Your Glory and all things for my good
So, let me express with all I have within me
Through the tears of joy, I want You now to see
As I sing to You

Chorus
Way Maker
Joy Giver
Peace Speaker
That's Who You are to me

My Healer
Strong Tower
Redeemer
That's Who You are to me.

Every generation, every century, man does what man does – follows the flesh and does his own thing. That's the "natural" thing to do... right? I always say we were not born bad – we all were born in sin but we learnt our ways according to the culture and situations we grew up in. And for some reason – it was and has always been more enticing to do the wrong thing.

At the heart of doing the "wrong thing" is the continuous search for finding who we really are. What am I here to accomplish? Why am I here? What is my purpose? We spend years developing a life timeline, trying to figure out where we truly belong when if we could just "get away into a quiet place – and grow in His presence" we would soon find the full purpose, mission, calling – the original plan for our limited stamp on the earth.

Our Creator had a plan in mind when He carved you and me out in our mother's womb. He wanted us to first be "little praisers – worshippers of Him – Jehovah God – warriors for Christ – contenders of the faith".

But we get distracted, wanting to fit in with the world more than get shut in with God. If the enemy can get us distracted long enough, we will miss out on our awesome God the Way Maker – who gives peace and joy – who heals and strengthens and redeems.

We continued in the time of worship. Every good song requires a bridge – right?! And again, as the Holy Spirit sang over us – I wrote and Brinton played... here comes the bridge...

Bridge
No matter where I go – You are there
You're never far away – You are there
You're so much more to me
You're all I'll ever need

So, I sing to You*...*

Chorus
Way Maker
Joy Giver
Peace Speaker
That's Who You are to me
My Healer
Strong Tower
Redeemer
That's Who You are to me.

How could this God – so amazing – love someone – so full of failure? Because He is Love. And His Love does not change, waver, nor can it be tampered with. The Word of God shows us in Romans 8:38-39 –

For I am persuaded, that neither death, nor life, nor angels, nor principalities, nor powers, nor things present, nor things to come, Nor height, nor depth, nor any other creature, shall be able to separate us from the love of God, which is in Christ Jesus our Lord. KJV

God's love for us is untouchable. Only we ourselves could change the outcome by not accepting His love. He is everywhere and in everything; He knows all and He sees all.

He is all we will really and truly ever need.
That writing experience for me was so exciting – so humbling

– so real! I wanted to write more – I was super excited... out of my experiences flowed a love song to Jesus; one I wanted everyone to hear and to live.

One that would become the theme song for the conference in Connecticut.

The first session for the conference came and we led the worship as was our assignment. Timid and wondering if our little song would be accepted, we ventured to sing the chorus. It caught on. And we were satisfied – at least temporarily.

Each session after that we added something else – the next session we did the verse and chorus.

And by the end of the conference the song was being sung by the attendants... the full song.

I was a nervous wreck at first but God showed us that He was in control and that He could use vessels who were available to Him... to bless others.

On the return to Jamaica, we quickly taught the group the song and ventured to sing it at Jamaica Youth For Christ's annual concert event to ring in the New Year – Genesis.

So now after all the prophecies and word of knowledge about me writing, it was happening – I was writing songs – again! But I wasn't prepared for the distraction ahead.

◆◆◆

NEW YEAR – NEW DISTRACTION

The year was still young. It could have been January or early

February – but we were still feeling a touch of the Christmas breeze.

Ping!

My phone alert went off.

A new video was out. Sinach was new to me and earlier in 2015 she came out with a "winning song" – the anthem of the Christian faith "I KNOW WHO I AM". I remember the night I first heard it – WOW!!!

We were at Salvation PhD, an annual concert held at the University of Technology in Kingston, Jamaica. A young man or was it a young man leading a group – I don't recall – but they did sing that song. I was the emcee. I could not stop singing the song about knowing who God says we are.

What A SONG!
Church start keep!

The concert went on but that chorus became a joy to sing. I could not wait to get to the radio station – Love 101 FM – to find the song and play it on air.

I played that song so many times.

I taught my worship team and every opportunity we had we sang that song. Before we knew it, every church, every child, every convention, and every youth meeting – everybody was singing "I KNOW WHO GOD SAYS I AM, WHAT HE SAYS I AM... "

So naturally with such a love and respect for this world class gospel minister, I had to follow her on social media and of

course I wanted to hear every other song she would sing.
So back to my PING!

It was a new song. Wait?! What?!

The name of the song... that looks familiar.

"Way Maker"?

I've got to hear this.

I hit play and there it was. I absolutely loved it... but there was
a *but*.

Two things were very familiar – the description of our Lord as
"Way Maker" and my line that says "That's Who You are to
me" – to her "That is Who You are".

I sank in my chair.

How now could I possibly SING MY SONG when this world
class, well beloved singer had a song with a similar theme?
Surely everyone would think I stole the idea from her.

I knew the truth. Kerina and Brinton knew the birth of that
song. Drs. Derek and Dorrett Senior also knew. And yes – the
Sweet Holy Spirit who inspired the song knew as well. But
would the world – well at least my "little" world believe?

I folded. I put the song away and went back to singing OPS –
"other people's songs".

Above the words of encouragement and the "big ups" – I was
deaf to it all. I just could not sing that song again.

It wasn't "good enough". It needed more. What would people say? What could they think? And the words of discouragement grew louder in my head.

I had thrown out all the reasons behind why this song was a good song.

Dr. Senior told me day in day out – hurry and record the song. My musicians were on my case. But nope. It was not to be so.

It was 2018 – about two and a half years later – when the Jamaica Gospel Music Network planned a meeting and I suggested we have my friend from London come and speak with the local gospel artistes. I wanted him to share his experiences and what he learnt on the ladder of success.

Noel Robinson is of Jamaican heritage and at the time was the only black Christian artiste based in London to be signed to Integrity Music of Don Moen fame.

THIS WAS BIG!!!

He was visiting family and the time was perfect for him to share.

Little did I know that God had big plans for me too.

◆◆◆

SING YOUR SONG

Noel shared some gems of the industry and I prayed the artistes were encouraged.

The Jamaica Gospel Music Network (JGMN) was an extension of another vision God had given to me and over the years of many ups and downs, it remained a struggle. Every now and again I wanted to just remind the gospel artistes of their worth and share information about how they could make the industry work for them. There's more on this JGMN journey in my next book – look out for it.

We were fascinated. Some things he shared, well, we could not do but it was good to hear. Some lessons were universal and could be applied to our situation in Jamaica.

The meeting had just about ended and Noel was just chit chatting and then he said it... not to anyone in particular and no, he was not speaking to me but when the words fell from his mouth they connected. The words spoke to a graveyard deep in my soul.

Out of the blue, I **overheard** Noel Robinson say "SING YOUR SONG!"

Whoa! Like a ton of bricks, it hit me. That's it, Nadine. Sing Your Song.

The Lord had taken the time and found you worthy to gift you with this song. SING YOUR SONG.

It has never left me. It took a while yet to really get the engine moving but I am getting the message... Sing my songs.

The God of this Universe downloads a gift – and this gift opened the door for the words to flow and the song came. There is something in it for someone – do not deprive them of that blessing.

It all made sense... but... still.

I had to laugh at my musicians. I am blessed to have had some of the best musicians playing for me since day one. My first stint in singing in a group was from when I was 10 years of age. And even back then I had the best of the best playing for me. Those stories are in my next book …by now you will get the message…get my next book too. (smiley face)

So here we are planning our 16th Anniversary special for Perpetual Sounds of Praise. I sent a list and we were getting ready for rehearsals. I walked into the studio – we prayed and I was ready to sing from my list.

My musicians totally ignored me – yes, me – their leader, and said "We are only doing originals". SING YOUR SONG.

I laughed. I had no time for "How dare you? It's my group!" They were right. So, we rehearsed most of the songs The Lord had allowed me to write... and what a catalogue. What memories! What a blessing.

You see, "Way Maker" was not the first song that I wrote. In fact, we already had an EP out with three of my originals and one from a former band member. Way Maker was just the first in a long time.

Johnoy, one of my tenors and a gospel artiste who goes by the name "GodArtiste", loves the second verse. He tells me that it is his favorite and how it has helped him through some dark times.

I am encouraged to hear that – so much so that often I let him take the lead on the second verse when the group sings.

Verse 2
I'm sure to grow when I am in Your presence

My will gets lost in Yours and I'm at peace
And no matter what I face I know the outcome
Is for Your Glory and all things for my good...

There have been others who have testified that this song has been a blessing. Dr. Senior has never forgotten that evening in his living room in Connecticut.

My desire is that persons will have that experience of finding a quiet place to worship at the feet of Jesus and out of those quiet times birth new ideas, new direction – newness. God is always filled with ideas – great ones too.

I don't remember who it was, but I remember the encouragement from a pastor friend. He pointed out that around the same period that I got that song, God was sending a message to the world that He can and will make a way. It was October 2015 that Travis Greene's album *The Hill* came out and on that album was the song "Made A Way". The conference we attended where God downloaded "Way Maker" was in November 2015 and it was about January 2016 that I saw the video from Sinach – "Way Maker".

Now my platform is in no way as big as theirs but when this pastor shared it... I felt encouraged. We later changed the name to "That's Who You are to Me" to stay away from distractions.

But all in all, so many lessons are to be learned from this story. Stop wasting time and tears – wishing and wondering. Choose to trust God. Stay in your God-given lane and do you! Be the best you – you can be... for Christ. And when we spend that time in His presence – seeking His face – hearing from Him what His perfect will is for each day, then... everything in this world – the distractions – the confusion will dim in the light of

His Glory.

I recently made a decision to really begin to SING MY SONG.

What is your song?

What is it that God has given to you – that thing that only YOU can do? Don't worry that your thing may not be to change the world. Focus on the fact that you too have a "thing" to do for Christ. And do it well.

Don't focus on the distractions. Each of us have a specific work to do and a work that we must answer to Christ about. I want to know that when I step before my King, He will know that I did everything I could to "Sing My Song" unto Him for the praise and glory of His name.

So now – with this in mind
With purpose in your focus
Throw away regrets of yesterday
And with a will that is robust
Turn your eyes on the Lord of your destiny
To whom your talents belong
Stay in your lane – do your thing
Whatever you do – Just SING YOUR SONG!!!

Written by Nadine Blair
NADSINK
July 24, 2019 – 11:59pm

Thanks to Jon Williams for the work on the score sheet for this song. I have a vision of Choirs all over singing this song. Join in the chorus…share it and sing along.

That's Who You Are to Me (Way Maker)

34
G/B
F/A
can find as- sur- ance His Word re- minds me
38 C/G
FMaj7
Am7
Dm7
F
this is not the end. Solo: So, I get a- way in- to my qui- et
43 G
Am7
Dm7
F
GSus7
place. And there I bask in His mer- cy and His grace_
48
49 C
G/B
F/A
_ and I say _ _ to Him. Choir: Way Ma- ker Joy giv- er Peace
54 C/G
F
F/A
G/B
C
Spea- ker That's who You are to me. My Hea- ler
59 G/B
F/A
C/G
F
F/A
G/B
Stong Tow- er Re- dee- mer That's who you are to me.
65 C
67 C
Solo: I am sure to grow when I am in your
69 G/B
F/A
C/G
C/E
pre- sence. My will gets lost in Yours and I'm at peace.
73 FMaj7
C
No mat- ter what I face see I al- rea- dy know

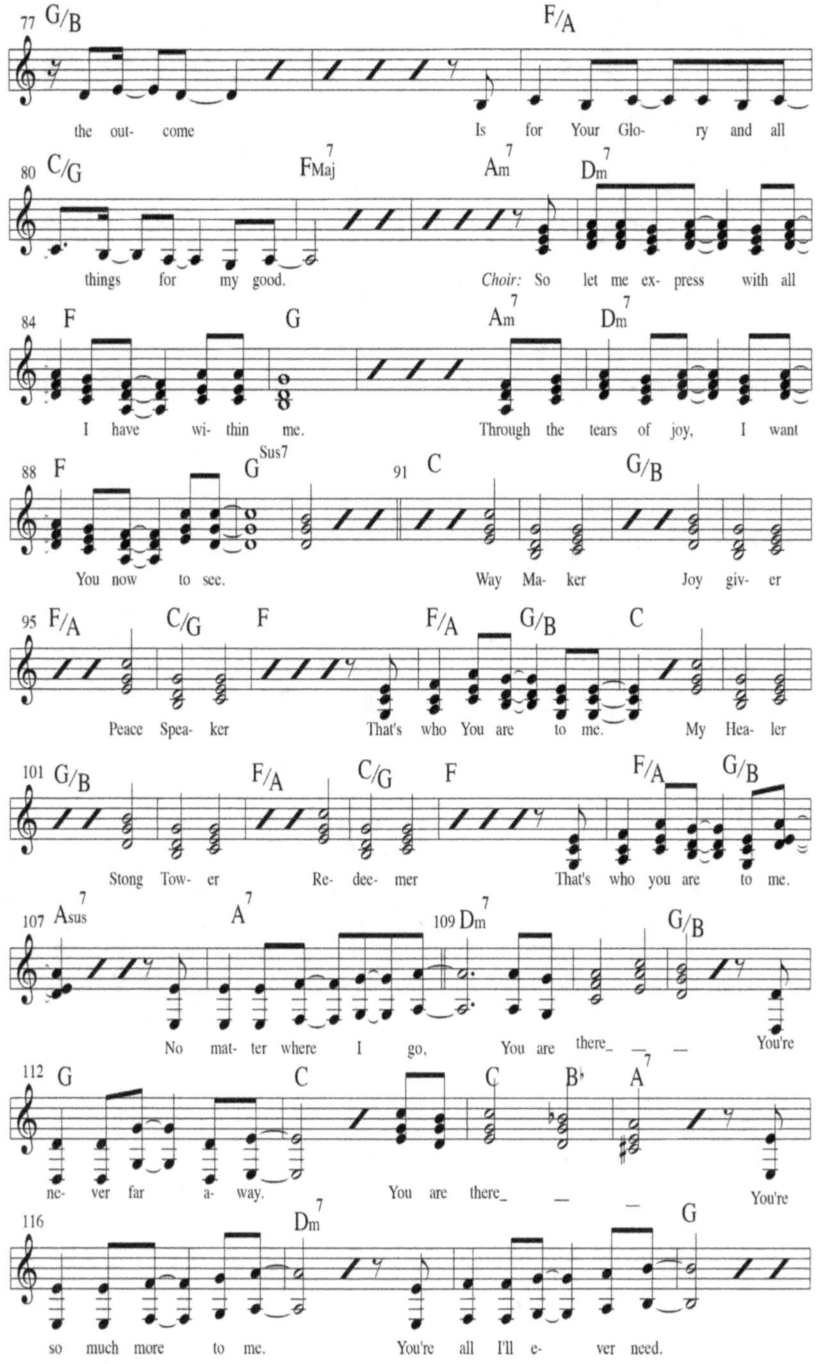

3
77 G/B
F/A
the out- come
Is for Your Glo- ry and all
80 C/G
F Maj7
Am7
Dm7
things for my good.
Choir: So let me ex- press with all
84 F
G
Am7
Dm7
I have wi- thin me.
Through the tears of joy, I want
88 F
G Sus7
91 C
G/B
You now to see.
Way Ma- ker
Joy giv- er
95 F/A
C/G
F
F/A
G/B
C
Peace Spea- ker
That's who You are to me.
My Hea- ler
101 G/B
F/A
C/G
F
F/A
G/B
Stong Tow- er
Re- dee- mer
That's who you are to me.
107 Asus7
A7
109 Dm7
G/B
No mat- ter where I go,
You are there_ _ _
You're
112 G
C
C
Bb
A7
ne- ver far a- way.
You are there_ _ _ _
You're
116
Dm7
G
so much more to me.
You're all I'll e- ver need.

120 E A/C# A
123 D F#Alt
So, I sing to You Way Ma-ker
125 Bm7 G F#m7 Bm7 Em7 G/B A/C#
Joy giv-er Peace Spea-ker That's who You are to me.
131 D A/C# G/B D/F#
My Hea-ler Stong Tow-er Re-dee-mer
137 G G/B A/C# 139 D A/C#
That's who you are to me. Way Ma-ker Joy giv-er
143 G/B D/A G G/B A/C# D
Peace Spea-ker That's who You are to me. My Hea-ler
149 A/C# G/B D/A G
Stong Tow-er Re-dee-mer That's
154 G/B A/C# D A/C# Bm7 D/A G D/F#
who you are to me. That's who you are to me. That's
158 Em7 A D F#Min Bmin D/A G Bm7
who you are to me. That's who you are to me. That's
162 Em7 A11 D
who you are to me.
2015 http://www.perpetualsoundsofpraise.com

Chapter 2
SING YOUR SONG - While You Wait

Waiting can be a pain if you don't train your mind to focus on the end result and not on the distractions.

It is amazing how we can get anxious and lose focus resulting in stress, depression, and other illnesses – just because we don't *"wait on the Lord: and be of good courage"*.

If you have ever received a word you must remember that that word can be for the immediate or for a time later – but if it is a word from the Lord – it will surely come to pass at the right time. We just need to wait.

In our humanness we, like Peter, forget to look straight into the eyes of Jesus and not allow the waves of life to pull our attention from Him. Jesus gave the command – "COME" and all Peter had to do was to set his face like a flint and keep moving no matter how high the waves were.

Fast forward to today... how many times have I? – Have *you?* – Have *we* – become frustrated because we are waiting for what seems to be years? One of many words spoken over my life was from Prophetess Maxine Johnson. Wow! I can't describe it; I just know that when the Prophetess had the entire church call my name out in the atmosphere, I knew something MUST shift on my behalf.

Did you hear it too? NADINE BLAIR – and they shouted together – in one voice – several times. We were in Orlando, Florida at the Deliverance Centre pastored by my uncle,

Bishop Herro Blair. It was Crusade time. And God had my name called out in the atmosphere.

I believe God for that breakthrough. Now the greater part of receiving a word is acting on it. And further I will speak about adding faith to the word.

Back in Jamaica and back at work, I got an assignment to do an interview with a Judge from South Florida. She shared how she too had received a word from the Lord that she would be a Judge. Of course, at first she did not believe but kept on doing what she loved to do and 10 years later – the word of the Lord came to fruition – she became a Judge... a respected woman of the Law in a land that did not birth her but one she pledged her allegiance to and is now serving with dignity. I almost fell out of my chair when she mentioned the name of the person who spoke the word.

So, God – You really trying to talk to me – eeeh?! Was this a reminder of the word He sent through His woman servant and also an encouragement to be patient in the wait? The same Prophetess Maxine Johnson who spoke the word over my life in Orlando a few weeks before the interview, was the same Prophetess who spoke over this judge's life.

The tears came and I remained still. He does *remember me.*

◆◆◆

HANNAH'S SONG

Do you remember the Bible story of Hannah?

Hannah was the favorite wife of Elkanah but she was unable to bear him a child. His other wife, Peninnah was pushing out babies like a factory. And with that Peninnah knew she had something over Hannah. Nah nah nah nah nah – I bet that was her song to Hannah. "A baay – me can have baby and you cyaa have none – a bay!" – Jamaican talk (I can have babies and you cannot have any!). That was Peninnah's song.

But what did Hannah do? What was Hannah's song?

How do you sing when your womb has been shut? The place of birthing has no hope of producing life? How do you sing when you are mocked for not bringing forth a dream?

I have had so many dreams, ideas, plans. Some I have carried out. Some I started and changed course because of negative influences. Talk truth, Nads!

I have come to realize that people will always talk. Some friends are really fren-emies; and some battles are just not worth fighting. It's simply not worth it. However, it does pay to find your musical bar and "buss a tune" to the King.

The Bible says *"... her (Hannah's) adversary also provoked her sore, for to make her fret..." (1 Sam. 1:6*, KJV). Sometimes you will literally be provoked to bits... and it's nothing more than to make you feel *less than*. You have to recognize the plan of the enemy and his "combolos" – those who choose to allow the enemy to use them, whether known to them or not.

The people are not your real enemy; however, if we are not careful, we can end up allowing ourselves to be used by him to cause pain on others. How can two who worship Christ together be at odds with one another – enough to not speak to one another? Ahh, but that's another chapter.

Let's get back to Hannah... What now became Hannah's song will change the trajectory of her life – the story being told today about Hannah is an encouragement to us. Hannah's song is written in history as one to follow.

Hannah waited and while she waited, she prayed. Her song was one of silence to the enemy's provocative words but one of hope in the Lord. Hannah must have sung a song like this>>>

"I will trust in the Lord no matter what I hear.
I will trust in the Lord; I won't bow to fear.
I will trust in the Lord whilst on this earth
I will trust in the Lord till I give birth".

Nowhere is it written that Hannah took it up on herself to respond to the distraction.

She waited – patiently.
She prayed – fervently.
She wept – bitterly.
She hoped – expectantly.

Hannah was getting ready to Sing her song. But it was not just any song – she added purpose and kingdom focus to her promise to God.

And she vowed a vow, and said, O Lord of hosts, if thou wilt indeed look on the affliction of thine handmaid, and <u>remember me</u>, and not forget thine handmaid, but wilt give unto thine handmaid <u>a man child</u>, then <u>I will give him unto the Lord all the days of his life</u>, and there shall no razor come upon his head."
(1 Sam. 1:11, KJV)

Hannah dared to make a vow. We have been taught that we are to be careful not to "run joke" with God and end up making a vow and not keeping it. Hannah went there. Her "song" started with a strong-willed determination to meet God half-way.

Hannah was specific in her request – she asked for a man child. She was not about to "waste time" and bear a female child; that would have been good but not great – not in those times when having a male child meant everything – the continuation of a lineage. And she added Kingdom value to her promise – she promised to give the child to God for His work.

And all it took was a confirming word from a man of God. In comes the Priest Eli – *"Then Eli answered and said, Go in peace: and the God of Israel grant thee thy petition that thou hast asked of him."* (1 Sam. 1:17, KJV)

Fast forward to that word that was spoken over your life... over my life... over that judge's life.

Hang on to that word, no matter how it seems that the word will not come to fore. Wait patiently but don't just sit there... do something. Pray! Fast! Find out what you need to do to see the dream come to pass.

Don't focus on the detractors nor the distractions. They will come! And sometimes from those closest to you. But while you wait, keep your eyes focused on Christ. Pray over your word. Make a commitment. Dare to believe God.

The best part of Hannah's story for me is found in verse 19: *"And they rose up in the morning early, and worshipped before the Lord, and returned, and came to their house to Ramah: and Elkanah knew Hannah his wife;*
*and **the Lord remembered her**"* (emphasis added).

And The Lord Remembered Hannah!

And the Lord remembered Nadine!

Put your name there.

And the Lord remembered _________!

While you wait – let your song be "I WILL TRUST IN THE LORD!!!!"

Don't be anxious.
Don't let your wait become a weight! – This was a theme God gave me for a singles conference years ago.

Don't let your wait become a weight!

– Nadine Blair

◆◆◆

ACHAN'S SONG LACKED WISDOM

Achan's song was very different. He became anxious and wanted too much too early. Lord, I pray that we will realize that waiting on You, Jehovah God, is always best for us.

In Joshua 6 we see where God gave specific instructions:

"Shout! For the Lord has given you the city! 17 The city and all that is in it are to be devoted to the Lord. Only Rahab the prostitute and all who are with her in her house shall be spared, because she hid the spies

> *we sent. 18* ***But keep away from the devoted***
> ***things, so that you will not bring about your own***
> ***destruction by taking any of them. Otherwise you***
> ***will make the camp of Israel liable to destruction***
> ***and bring trouble on it. 19 All the silver and gold***
> ***and the articles of bronze and iron are sacred to***
> ***the Lord and must go into his treasury.***"
> (Emphasis added) (NIV)

This was to be the first war after they had marched around the walls of Jericho together, shouted together, and claimed the new land together.

You would think that after all of this walking through the desert for years, planning the big invasion and seeing the walls come down that they would all be on the same page.

Achan became a little anxious.

Let us examine the instructions. God specifically said do not touch the devoted things and He said what would happen – destruction and trouble. Now who would have wanted a clearer set of instructions?

Jehovah God further said all the gold and silver belong to Him. Touch not.

Achan became impatient. *Why wait when I can have some now?*

Is that what we say when faced with an option to take what does not belong to us? To "taste" a bit of the "forbidden fruit" now rather than wait? To test the waters before marriage? To hurry a response – reacting rather than responding?

We can learn so much in the wait.

There's another song that the Lord gave me in a studio. Pastor Dean Smith is an anointed pastor and gifted song writer. He and his wife Prophetess Sarah Smith pastor Light of the Gentiles International and I have the utmost respect for them. Amazing people.

Whilst in studio one day, Pastor Dean was singing a chorus the Lord had given him...

CHORUS
You deserve Oh God!
You deserve Oh God!
You deserve Oh God!
More than I can give
So, here's my everything!

We later changed "give" to "**bring**" as suggested by Babbie Mason in a songwriter's session on the Logos Hope ship.

As I think about Achan and Hannah and so many other examples in the Word and in my time... the answer to the impatient bug is just being still.

As Pastor Dean sang – I grabbed my pen and wrote what I heard in the Spirit...

VERSE
It's so easy to be distracted
By what life has to bring
Got to get myself together
To worship You my King
What's the use if I'm too busy
Doing what You called me to

When I don't take the time to focus
Or even spend some time with You?

It is easy to imagine that Achan got distracted by the sparkly stuff. When they went to war all the rules that God had laid down went through the door. And Achan forgot who he was and what his purpose was.

Achan was from the great and powerful tribe of Judah. Oh, if he could see into the future to see what God had in store for Him – just around the bend.

Joshua and the Israelites were sure they would have conquered Ai. But something went wrong. They lost that battle... and miserably too.

When they did their checks, it was revealed that the fault lay somewhere in the tribe of Judah. What an indictment! What irony! In the Tribe of where? Judah!!!

The punishment? They were stoned to death – the entire family. God don't play. Achan decided he would take what belonged to God and hide it. He disobeyed a direct command and, as God had warned, brought failure in battle on the nation. Achan took the things that did not belong to him – they were first fruits to God.

And what made it worse is that he took them and could not even use them; he had to hide them. What relationship are we entertaining that we know something is wrong with this picture – If we can't show him off... if we can't bring her to a public setting – why bother?

Don't let your wait become a weight.

Let your song be *"They that wait upon the Lord shall renew their strength."*[1]

The story of Achan gets more interesting. Because of his disobedience all of Israel suffered – they lost a battle and ultimately Achan and all his family were stoned to death and their belongings destroyed. We are all connected. And your failure to be still before God... my failure to wait patiently upon His timing... our failure to want what is best for each of us - can affect someone else.

Here is the most interesting thing about this story with Achan: these are the instructions from the Lord for when they were to again face Ai. Jehovah God said in Joshua chapter 8:

> 1 *"Then the Lord said to Joshua, "Do not be afraid; do not be discouraged. Take the whole army with you, and go up and attack Ai. For I have delivered into your hands the king of Ai, his people, his city and his land. 2 You shall do to Ai and its king as you did to Jericho and its king, except that **you may carry off their plunder and livestock for yourselves**. Set an ambush behind the city."* (Joshua 8:1-2, NIV; Emphasis added)

Wait on the Lord and in due time you will get all you need for the journey – for your life. Wait, I say, on the Lord.

If Achan had just

- waited one more day
- fought one more battle
- overcome one more trial

---

[1] See Isaiah 40:31 (KJV).

\-   walked in obedience one more time...

he would have been alive and could have been a part of that celebration.

What will your song be while you wait?

Let us first strive to stay in His presence and in our lane. To choose to please Him – listening keenly for His direction and His word and acting there upon it. And while you wait, don't watch the distractions – don't get hasty and pick up what does not belong to you. SING YOUR SONG – WHILE YOU WAIT.

And so, I wait...

Finding myself in the meantime... I wait

Searching the mirror for signs of yesterday that have become
heavy weight
Leaving myself at God's beck and giving Him my all
A surgical procedure necessary to withdraw
The baggage, the masks, - the unfinished tasks
That led me to meddle - in relationships left unsettled.

God as I wait – do what You must
Move me from faith in the waiting to simple trust
For I cannot proceed until this need
To be who You've called me to be –
Is in my heart and mind – understood
My purpose, my place – You are working for my good

And what if You choose who in my eyes
I don't desire?
What if You've called me to walk alone on this mire?
What if the wait becomes longer and brings greys to my

head;
As the lesson for me to learn unfolds...
What if I see my own way out instead?

What if the pain is too much to explain?
No one may want me and my past to bear.
What if my "what if's" come in the way,
And block my heart from what I need to hear?

Then You say if only I be still
"Don't let your wait become a weight"
– pray until
You say the lesson is bigger than the blessing
So, I now must focus on what I may be missing
It is in You that I stand complete
It is in You I have all I need
It is in You – I am ready to face
My purpose, my destiny, my place

And so, I wait

Written by Nadine Blair April 7, 2008 for Singled Out Singles Conference hosted by Nadine Blair & Allowed To Shine Ministries

Chapter 3
SING YOUR SONG – Even When Life Gets Bitter

I almost started to cry at the thought of it... *God thinks our tears are special.* Well, wouldn't that make you want to just "tear up" a little more?!

I don't know if there is a literal bottle but Psalm 56:8 (KJV) says:

> *8 Thou tellest my wanderings: put thou my tears into thy bottle: are they not in thy book?*

This for me means Jehovah God is mindful of our pain – and especially if we suffer for His sake.

Revelation 5:8 KJV says:

> *"And when he had taken the book, the four beasts and four and twenty elders fell down before the Lamb, having every one of them harps, and golden vials full of odours, which are the prayers of saints."*

Odours here does not refer to stench – or stink smell but rather incense – the incense that rises to the throne room when we cry before The Lord."

Our tears are important to God.

It was a beautiful thought that birthed into a song of worship before the Lord. ***The God of this Universe is concerned when I cry***.

And there have been many an instance when the tears did flow.

But who is thinking about God collecting tears when you are in the middle of a sea of disappointment? Maslow's Hierachy of Needs shows that we are supposed to "graduate" from one level of need to the next. But I often wonder what would happen if you are stuck at the social need rung on that ladder.

You see, Maslow thought that we move from physiological needs – the basic need of water, food, warmth, and rest to the security needs – that of safety and security. We all need that.

The next rung on the ladder is the social need, which applies to friends and intimate relationships.

The last two are esteem and self-actualization.

But what if we feel like we can't genuinely move from social needs to the next because of failed friendships – over and over again? Would there be an external or internal reasoning behind the inability of creating and maintaining strong social friendship circles? In my capacity of a public figure on a lower scale, I have seen them all: the friends who mean you well but somehow disappoint; the friends who attach themselves to gain what they can; the friends who are true from beginning to the end.

What do you do when friends fail? Sing your song. I've had many occasions of curling up in my bed and praying one by one, name by name, situation by situation, all for those friends who hurt me to the core. Sometimes you have to gather the strength to simply walk away.

Soul searching is always good. I tell people, start looking on the inside first. If you hear a comment targeted at you – first ask "Is it true? Are there things I need to change or address?" If the answer to these questions is yes, then you start the process, learn from the mistake, do whatever needs to be done, and keep moving.

> *The God of this Universe is concerned*
> *when I cry.*

It makes no sense for you to sit and allow the negative to overtake you. You will win if you look at it as a learning opportunity. Cry if you must – in fact, draw for some songs of repentance in scripture like Psalm 51. And if the shoe did not fit then sing the song of Psalm 43 or 26. But don't you dare go into hiding and allow the pain to swallow you up.

> The Message Bible – Psalm 43:1-2
> *Clear my name, God; stick up for me*
> *against these loveless, immoral people.*
> *Get me out of here, away*
> *from these lying degenerates.*

> The Message Bible – Psalm 26:1
> *Clear my name, God;*
> *I've kept an honest shop.*
> *I've thrown in my lot with you, God, and*
> *I'm not budging*

It is true that how you respond comes with maturity. Experience has taught me not to cry over certain situations – deal with the hurt head-on. Sometimes you won't be able to speak to the accuser. Sometimes you won't know who it is.

Sometimes your very life will be threatened – yes. But do you know your God? Then sing your song.

In life we have options – we can react or we can respond. I tell my friends – learn to respond. A response requires you to STOP – think – process – then make an informed, calculated response to an attack or accusation or even a suggestion. Sometimes we may even have to pray before responding.

A reaction is impulsive and may find you reacting to a misunderstood statement. Allow the Holy Spirit time to guide and a place to lead you and even though you may still feel disappointed when we act according to His leading – we will find that the resultant position is always best for all.

I've been in a recurring nightmare of misunderstandings. One particular case where someone heard something about me and chose to believe resulted in the person literally shutting me off. We might have ended up in a church setting, worshipping the same God, but they were not having it – they were not speaking to me at all. What did I choose to do? Sing my song.

It got so bad that I would be on stage and the person would sit in the front row and be noticeably agitated. What did I do? I prayed for them... good things. Thank God for that particular situation right now I can say we are good...we talked – we prayed – we good.

That scenario is a recurring one – one that I face so often. Someone hears something and they don't bother to check the facts – and their actions towards me would be those of disgust.

My parents taught me well. Ha! I remember a situation where my father was fought – in church! Yes – he was transferred to a church; some of the folk did not want him to be the pastor and one night he went during a Bible study I believe – or was it prayer meeting? They turned off the lights and "buss a fight" on my father INSIDE THE CHURCH.

What did my dad do? What did my mother do? "Oh, the Lord will fight for us – don't worry – it will work out!"

"Yeah, right!" was my thinking... but they had their song. I remember hearing them singing to Dottie Rambo's "Thank You for the Valley," a song which speaks about rejoicing even in dark, unexpected situations. My parents found their song in the dark and lit it up with their praise.

The Psalmist was right – Just HOW can you sing when you are in a strange land? Psalm 137:4

But yes – I have watched my parents find their song in the middle of their darkest hour. I have heard them pray for their enemies and seen them do good to persons who spitefully use them. I have heard them SING THEIR SONG.

No wonder – even though I wanted to fight for them then – I grew to understand the power of my song in worship to God, in the middle of my greatest pains.

The recurring dream, the familiar spirit, the continuous drama always comes to an end when I find my song. I pray in earnest for the accuser. I may keep my distance when danger is present – and oh yes, there have been those times when the law has had to come into play (that's another book), but my rule of thumb is to try my utmost – to pray for my enemies and genuinely mean them the best. I do my best to keep my heart pure.

And most times – if not all – God gets the big GLORY and the person comes into an understanding of "Oops!" and we are good after that. I tell you this – that even if it does not end well; our stance must always be – "Be Still" and KNOW that God is in control.[2] And pray – yes, pray! – for our accusers.

You see, the enemy will make us believe that the person is the real enemy. But oh no. We have one common enemy – and it is sad that many times persons don't realize that they have allowed that enemy to use them to sow discord.

Lord, open our eyes – and help us realize. We are better united in this fight. We don't have to agree on everything, but we must love.

There were nights I would cry myself to sleep. Wondering - what did I do wrong? What I said wrong. Or just what I had missed. And then the morning light would come with me back on air on the radio smiling for the world but hurting inside. It's the life of the public figure – to smile even when it hurts. For our lives don't really belong fully to us.

- ∂   *Our purpose is higher than our pain.*
- ∂   *Our mission bigger than our mess.*
- ∂   *Our duty larger than our disappointments.*
- ∂   *We are in this for the greater good.*

Don't get me wrong – we must pause to heal, for an aching doctor is no good to his patients. And just as the very psychologist has their own psychologist – and the doctor has their own doctor to see too... so too each of us must find that time to heal if there is the need.

––––––––––––––––––––––––

[2] See Psalm 46:10.

On the plane the air hostess will tell you, "Place the mask over your nose first. Then you may attend to others." There we go again. SING YOUR SONG. For how can we in our pain fix the needs of those around us?

Our purpose is higher than our pain.

Our mission bigger than our mess.

Our duty larger than our disappointments.

– Nadine Blair

It may be argued that we should always lend an ear and help even when we are without. That is true. But there comes a time when you must – you have to – you *betta* – lock away and heal. In His presence and at a spa if you can. LOL – it just makes sense.

There is a song that came to me from a deep, deep place. I don't quite remember the circumstances that brought the song; I just remember driving and hearing the words and they flowed...:

CHORUS
Healing Jesus, heal my heart
Take away the pain
Healing Jesus, heal my heart
Revive my soul again
Healing Jesus – Heal me
Healing Jesus – Heal me

A few days later we were slated to minister in Montego Bay – Nadine Blair & Perpetual Sounds of Praise. I taught my band the song –just the part I had heard in my spirit up to then. On the way to the event, the verses came right there on the bus. At the time of my writing this book, I have only sung the full song once. I took my time to explain to the audience how the song came.

But never did I expect the response I saw. There were tears and the altar was full. The stories I heard after melted my heart. To this day I keep in touch with one of those who came to the altar. Fay's story was one of heartbreak and the song was meant for her.

VERSE 1
If I had the chance to live my life all over
I would try my best mistakes never to make
I'd remind my heart that trials make me stronger
Little is much when God is in the midst.
So, while I'm here and facing disappointments
Lord help me to be steadfast And not give in
So, hear me now as I cry with my whole being
Only You Lord can deliver
Hear my plea

CHORUS 1
Healing Jesus, heal my heart
Take away the pain
Healing Jesus, heal my heart
Revive my soul again
Healing Jesus – Heal me
Healing Jesus – Heal me

Second Corinthians 1:4 says *"He comforts us in all our*

troubles so that we can comfort others. When they are troubled, we will be able to give them the same comfort God has given us." (NLT)

What you are going through is not just for you. In this world, we will face challenges – trials, temptations, disagreements, hurt, disappointment, and the list goes on. But if we know and understand and try to remember this one thing... we can boldly go to God and express, cry, pray, let our requests be made known – just talk to Him. And He promises to bring us that comfort we so desperately need.

My dad preached recently and I will borrow a line from his message about Jacob.

"He had comfortable sleep in an uncomfortable situation." – Bishop Dr. Ronald Blair

Here is Jacob all messed up – living the life of a trickster who was himself eventually tricked. And yet God's hand was still on him. God still heard his cry. God still healed his heart.

Desperate and afraid, he sent everyone away and became *"A Seeking man – Alone with God"* (that was dad's title for his message – wow!!!).

Sometimes that is what it takes for us to get what we really need. Searching, struggling, strength-deprived, and just plain "salt" (as we would say in Jamaica) but it is in this place we can be heard by God, who bottles up our tears, binds up our wounds, heals our aching heart, and gives us comfort in the midst of "WHATEVER" – so that when we meet someone who is facing the same or similar situation, we can say "I KNOW EXACTLY WHAT YOU MEAN and here is my story of how I got over by God's grace."

> *"He had comfortable sleep in an uncomfortable situation."*
>
> *~ Bishop Dr. Ronald Blair*

The situation may differ, but the pain may very well be relatable. Pain is Pain. Hurt is Hurt. But find your song and sing it loud. My friend could not quantify her pain – she could not give it a number on the "Rip-ter" scale (pun intended)... the pain that "rips" your heart out, but she knew pain. And she could relate. Here is verse two:

VERSE 2

Can't describe just how it feels when I am hurting
When the words escape my lips – I can't believe
For when friends and those close to me take great pleasure
To try to bring me down or block my destiny

Lord, You know what it's like to be disappointed
I do that to You time and time again
For every heartbreak that I bring to You
You know the real deal
And You love me back into Your arms again

CHORUS 2

Healing Jesus – Heal my heart
Take away the sin
Healing Jesus – Heal my heart
Cleanse me from within
Healing Jesus – Heal me
Healing Jesus – Heal me

My prayer for me – for you – for us, is that we will have a daily revelation of God. There is so much in Him that we won't get bored. Have you ever read a Bible verse and gotten a deep understanding and months, years later when you read it again you get a different revelation?

God's ability to heal is only limited by our faith to believe.

And God is able. Able to heal and deliver. This mighty awesome God who gives us songs in the night where doom and gloom dwell, is singing over us and invites us to join in... He will deliver. He will heal. He will sort it out. As Morgie (a Jamaican gospel artiste) would sing – "God a guh fix it up tomorrow" (God will fix this situation tomorrow).

Our Jehovah Rophe mends hearts and broken relationships, and He heals minds and bodies too. It is never too much. Never too late. Never too complicated. Don't limit what God can do.

Our tears matter to God. There is a saying that goes something like this: "Don't let Mama's tears catch you" – I want to think that Mama be praying to God... and that is what one should watch out for. When God 'hears' your tears.

Whenever I am faced with that situation of what people say and think, etc. I take out what is applicable to me and discard the rest. And I pray... good things for my fren-emies and enemies, leave the rest to God, and 'SING MY SONG'.

We don't have to receive in our spirit –
what persons say in the natural!

~ Nadine Blair

God's ability to heal is only limited by our faith to believe!

~ Nadine Blair

Chapter 4
SING YOUR SONG – Break the Chains with Your Praise!

The children of Jehovah God are blessed with so much – we have direct access to this awesome and powerful God. Thanks be to Jesus Christ we can go into the Holy of Holies – the very presence of God and make our petitions known.

So why are we walking around in the desert of life waiting for the next seminar or conference to get a booster vaccination that we allow to die out anyway as our pseudo-motivated spirit gets a reality check when hit with the arrows of the real war that's going on – the war for our souls?

In his book *The Power of Praise & Worship* Terry Law outlines the finest weapons for any man in any century. (*Great book by the way – you should read it.*) God has blessed us, endowed us, imparted unto us the wonderful book – the best seller – THE B.I.B.L.E. our "**b**asic **i**nstructions **b**efore **l**eaving **e**arth" (source unknown).

Yes, some of our weapons are God's WORD, the name of Jesus, and the Blood of Jesus and I will add…our Praise.

Gain all the knowledge you can by reading the WORD OF GOD, studying the use of the NAME OF JESUS and how to apply the BLOOD OF JESUS. Gain all the KNOWLEDGE you can to KNOW your weapons, then ask for UNDERSTANDING to know HOW to use them and ask the Holy Spirit for WISDOM to know WHEN to use these weapons.

There is dynamite power when we use these weapons in praise and worship.

What will your response be to your next trial? Will you curl up and fret? Roll over and die? Or will you, with all your might, find your weapon and use it in praise to Jehovah God?

◆◆◆

Let's Talk Weapons

THE WORD

Why is this weapon so powerful? Well, first of all it is God-breathed and Holy Spirit-delivered. You don't want much more than that for an explanation. I remember one night after my dad had a stroke – thank God it was not debilitating... but it affected his eyes. So, reading for Dad has become a chore – and my dad *loves* to read. He called me in to read for him. I took up the Word and began to read. It was "just a few Psalms" – nothing much really... ha!!! So I thought.

Before long, while I was reading, the tears were flowing. And I know you are going to say it's because I love to cry. No. There was just something beautiful about the Word of God. How precious when read aloud. Try it!

Some may say they don't like reading the parts of the Bible that are just a bunch of names listed for genealogy purposes. It's amazing to me that in a list of names that were 'chronicled' so precisely in 1 Chronicles 4, all of a sudden (it would seem), there would be a verse about a man who said a prayer that has become an anthem around the world to this day. Books have been written about this verse – the man and his prayer –

songs have been penned and soloists and choirs alike belt out the words with much faith and fervor – OH THAT GOD WOULD BLESS ME INDEED.

And then just like that verse 11 picks up again with the listing of names.

You never know what you might get from reading the Bible – anywhere – it is so precious. It WILL change your life.

Even persons who perform evil works know there is power in the WORD. Some even walk with the New Testament in their back pockets. So those who call the name of Christ must know and believe this Word.

My mom is an effervescent preacher... my dad is the teacher and my mom will rage war in her messages. She's something else. But once I heard her say – or was it while she was praying? – ***"If God did not want us to believe it, He would not have put it in the Bible." (– Rev. Evon Blair).***

WOW!!! Talk about lightbulb moment. Every promise in His Word is TRUE. Every Word – Yes and Amen – and His Amen is in Christ. What Christ did for us makes it all possible.

So again, I say, God's ability to heal, God's ability to deliver – to set free – to move – will be limited to our believing and moving on His word. There will be times when God will just DO IT! But there are so many times He just wants us to believe Him AND make the move. Rev. Clinton Chisholm once said "Move Your Lap" – you know that thought where we expect things to just drop in our laps? Well, there are times when we will have to "move our laps" – make a move on what God has said.

Make a move standing on His Word.

"If God did not want us to believe it, He would not have put it in the Bible."

~ Rev. Evon Blair

THE NAME – JESUS CHRIST, SON OF THE LIVING GOD!

It is amazing what understanding will do. There are those who have the knowledge – they know the words of the Bible; they may even have met the God of the Bible, but don't have an understanding of the power that they can access. I really should say "we" – because Lord knows sometimes, I forget – honestly.

That world anthem which was written and first sung by Will Reagan and later redone by Tasha Cobbs Leonard, says it – so simply put "There Is Power In the Name of Jesus."

How many times do we see this reference to the Name of Jesus in the Bible?

Proverbs 18:10 NKJV says: *"The name of the LORD is a strong tower; the righteous run to it and are safe."*

I imagine His Name as this mighty place of safety. Sometimes just a whisper of His Name is all we need. And He comes, He answers, and He runs to us. There are many who call on Him out of habit... you buck your toe, "Jesus!"; a fender bender – "Jesus!"; in the heat of an argument "Jesus!" Deep down, we know!!!!

Sadly, there are situations where knowing His name and **Understanding** the power behind His name are so far apart – grandma's teeth have nothing on us. Smile.

Even the demons know and understand the power in His name. So why not us?

◆◆◆

THE BLOOD

The significance of blood is understood in the dark world more than we know. In the Bible, from the beginning of time, we see where the shedding of blood was intricate in sacrifice. The priests had to take blood from an unblemished lamb and take that to offer up – the cleansing power came when all was acceptable – even the priest himself.

In comes Jesus, and after His death and the shedding of His blood, the veil was torn and everything changed.

It is now a faith walk. A one-to-one communication – direct to the Throne Room – every man for himself.

Jesus' blood changed everything.

By faith I can plead the blood against or I can apply the blood on or to. So, I plead the blood against you, Satan. and I apply the blood of Jesus on my mind and my body and believe God for my healing.

There is power in our weapons – nothing can stand against us when we, with faith, use the Word of God, the Name of Jesus, and the Blood of Jesus.

◆◆◆

WEAPON OF PRAYER

It hit me and I was like – oh yes – for real…Our prayers are weapons. So when we feel tired and would rather just lie there, maybe roll over and draw the covers for another snooze… sometimes my friend, God is calling us into conversation with Him and that is a weapon.

How could we miss this simple yet most effective weapon? We get to go into the Holy of Holies – forget having to get a lamb, a goat or whatever animals they used to bring to the Priest back then. The veil was torn and we now have access.

This access means we can talk to the One who holds eternity in His hands. This is like a big huge WOW! We can talk to The Father and share all we are going through, all our feelings, everything.

But it would be rather one sided if it ended there – right? But you see it doesn't. Prayer is not just access – but it is access to conversation. This means The Father – Jehovah God – takes the time to answer. You might hear it in a soft whisper; or a steady feeling of peace. Maybe someone will call and share something that is just up your alley and what you needed to hear.

Yes, prayer brings access to and acknowledgement from the Almighty God. And with this dialogue you must know it is not limited to that time in church when we all bow to pray; or when we are home and kneel in humble reverence; but prayer can also be an on-going conversation. In your car, at your office, walking to the bus stop – anywhere you are.
"…men ought always to pray, and not to faint…" Luke 18:1 KJV

We must maintain, nurture and press to always pray and never give up.

"…Pray without ceasing!" 1 Thessalonians 5:17 – KJV

Missionary Scott, one of my faithful listeners on Love 101 FM, puts it right when she said to me one day – "Auntie Nadine – we must learn to pray and put down" – meaning – before the trials come, before the pain comes, before disappointment comes – when it is all nice and dandy – Pray! When things look like they are all going your way – practice the principle of prayer – daily, constant – especially the "late-in-the-midnight-hour" type of prayer.

For when the battle rages – you may not feel as if you have the strength to pray or praise. But because you have put some up in the prayer bank – that my friend is what will keep you.

So yes, pray! Pray for the people who let you down. Pray for strength to turn your frown upside down in the midst of gut wrenching – heart breaking pain. Use your weapon of Prayer and communicate with the God of the ages.

Pray on!

◆◆◆

NOW LET'S TALK PRAISE

I don't know when my love for praise really began. As a child I was lead singer for a singing group. That story is in another book coming to a shelf – virtual or otherwise – near you.

What I have learnt over the years is that the simple truth is that God made us to praise Him, and as the enemy sees us in our mother's womb as a "potential praiser of Christ" – he will do anything to stop that praise. So, our praise IS important. Our praise is "valued by God" and "envied by Satan".

By our pure praise we open the door for God to fight for us. With our praise the answers come. As the sound of a sweet symphony in your ear, so is the sound of our genuine praise in the ears of our loving Father. And He fights for us... God our Mighty Warrior will rise from His throne and stop the plans of the enemy. This is what our praise does.

◆ ◆ ◆

WHEN GOD DOWNLOADS A NEW SONG ON THE SPOT!

It was at our 17th Anniversary Celebration that this song came.

We were close to the end of the "live on social media" in-studio-session. My parents were there. I was so happy they came... and stayed. And even with the loudness they worshipped and rocked and sang along all night.

Then I heard the first line – "Yes, I overcome..." That's all I heard. And doubt stepped in.

You see, I am still weaning myself from the "Don't Sing your Song Syndrome". Naa lie! I have had so many prophesies about me writing songs. And I'm like "yeah, right" – "sure" – "whatever man."

But then the songs started to come.

Even so, it's a totally different thing when you are on stage, live, in front of an audience and you hear words singing in your mind.

The natural thing to do is doubt. *Maybe I can write it later when I am more focused. What if I start singing and nothing else follows?*

I invite you to visit my YouTube Channel and you will see the video for yourself. (Nadine Blair YouTube Channel – please like & subscribe – smile) I started by saying *"If I stay here..., I hear songs all the time."*

It was singing over me... and I had to step out in faith. So, I started...

"Yes, I overcome... (then I heard) ... by the power of The Blood"

And then Dawn Martin joined in on the third time around and Kareem Haynes on the fourth. The rest of the singers joined in. The harmony was beautiful.

The musicians were clueless, but it was evident that this was bigger than all of us. None of us had ever heard the song before. It was brand-new to me, definitely brand-new to the singers, and most definitely never played before by the musicians.

God was in the midst of us. And He was singing over us.

I was thinking – OK then, what next? Every musician/singer knows you can't just keep singing one line over and over "jus' so-so suh." You need a bridge or something to lift the song.

Then Wendell dropped the beat and immediately I heard...

"I'm breaking chains with my praise – yeah"

And that was the essence of it. The big message. We break chains with our praise.

◆◆◆

TESTIMONY TIME

My mom told the story (sooooo many times – lol) of how she was having a pain and nothing would help. She could not lie down; she could barely move sometimes. One day she went to prayer. Then she started to praise. I don't know exactly what she said but she said she praised God so much she forgot where she was and eventually, she fell asleep, right on the carpet.

When she woke up, she got up immediately – she did not remember about the pain. It was after a while she thought to herself – "But wait, I got up without any help and I am not in pain." Her praise had reached God's heart and broken the chain of pain.

Why not stop right now and begin to worship Jehovah God? With understanding!! John 4:23-24 says –

23 But the hour cometh, and now is, when the true worshippers shall worship the Father in spirit and in truth: for the Father seeketh such to worship him. 24 God is a Spirit: and they that worship him must worship him in spirit and in truth. (KJV)

I love the Message Bible's interpretation of this:

"It's who you are and the way you live that count before God. **Your worship must engage your spirit in the pursuit of truth.** That's the kind of people the Father is out looking for: those who are simply and honestly *themselves* before him in their worship. God is sheer being itself—Spirit. Those who worship him must do it out of their very being, their spirits, their true selves, in adoration." (John 4:23-24 MSG)

Did you get it?

"Your Worship must engage your spirit in the pursuit of truth"

Don't just say the words because you know them; let it flow from your heart with understanding. Your worship – the act of worship – the words you say, the hands being raised, everything we do in worship – must engage our spirit as we pursue Christ.

Praise Him with understanding. Know what you mean when you say:

"Jehovah God, I adore You,"
"I lift You up,"
"Thank You Jesus"
"Lord Jesus I magnify Your Name"

What are you **really** saying? What do you mean when you say it? Think about what you are singing and go beyond a robotic recital of words and really connect with God.

Praise Him without expectations – just praise Him because *He is.* Praise Jehovah God whether you are feeling great or you are feeling down. Praise Him for His grace and for His mercy. Praise God from whom ALL blessings flow. Praise God in the midst of whatever you are facing.
Chained to a prison cell (literal or mental)?
SING YOUR SONG to Jehovah God
Marriage on the rocks and you want it firmly standing on the rock Christ Jesus?

SING YOUR SONG to Jehovah God

Children out of line and they have forgotten everything you taught them?
SING YOUR SONG to Jehovah God

Workplace issues – they don't even recognize you?
SING YOUR SONG to Jehovah God

Whatever the situation…
Whatever the battle…
Whatever the storm…
SING YOUR SONG to Jehovah God.

Paul and Silas had options. Here are these great men of God called and committed to Christ. So why should they decide to sing knowing that God could have turned the tide and not have them locked up in prison? Sometimes life will not be fair. People will lie on you. Friends will fail you. Boss will overlook you. That is life.

But in this prison, chained and bound, Paul and Silas found their song and they began to sing.

Maybe they were singing this song:

"I'm breaking chains with my praise – yeah!"

Or maybe they were singing one of my favorite hymns:

My Hope is built on nothing less
Than Jesus Blood and righteousness
I dare not trust the sweetest frame
But wholly lean on Jesus' name

On Christ the Solid Rock I stand
All other ground is sinking sand
All other ground is sinking sand
Edward Mote (1834)

And God heard their praise... and I imagined that God stood up.

Maybe that's what caused the place to shake and the chains to break. Wonderful things happen when our pure praise hits the ears of a pleased God and He responds.

GLORY BE TO THE MOST HIGH GOD

JEHOVAH GOD, YOU ARE WORTHY!!!!

We were singing the two lines back and forth and once again my drummer, Wendell, dropped the beat and immediately, again, I heard:

"He gave me a new name,
And I'm no longer the same"

And just like that, the song was completed. Three lines, but that was all we needed. This song was totally orchestrated by God, in the moment, on the spot. WOW!!!

BREAKING CHAINS WITH MY PRAISE

Yes, I overcome, by the Power of The Blood

I'm Breaking Chains with my Praise yeah!

He gave me a New Name, And I'm no longer the same!

Inspired by The Holy Spirit
- Written by Nadine Blair

Just before the recording session for this song, I heard more words – and so the recorded version will have a reprise with verses. But the main song itself bore three lines that each tell a powerful story.

Know the power that is in your praise.
Know the power you have within you.
Know your God and SING YOUR SONG.

My mom is a real prayer warrior. One day we decided to write what God is to us using each letter of the alphabet. It is something we use on occasion – and we have a shorter list posted in our Prayer Grotto at home. (Yes, as Marion Hall says in her song, there is definitely "A room at our house prepared for Jesus").

I will share some of those words with you – you can create your own list and use them in prayer. It's amazing when you think about what Jehovah God has done for you; what Christ Jesus did on Calvary – and put a praise on your situation.

An Alphabetical Guide of Praise

A – Amazing, Able, Attentive, Anointed One
B – Beautiful, Bountiful, Beginning, Bread of Life
C – Caring, Capable, Compassionate, Creator
D – Divine, Deliverer, Dependable
E – Excellent, El-Shaddai, Everlasting Father
F – Faithful, Forgiving, Friend, Father
G – God, Good, Great, Gracious, Guardian
H – Help, Holy, Hallowed, Healer, Hope
I – Indescribable, Incomparable, Intentional
J – Just, Jealous, Judge
K – Kind, King, Keeper
L – Love, Lord, Light, Life, Life-Giver
M – Master, Mighty, Marvelous, Messiah, Merciful
N – Near, Nurturer
O – Omnipotent, Order, Omniscient, On-Time, Omnipresent
P – Powerful, Patient, Protector, Peace, Pure
Q – Quick
R – Redeemer, Refuge, Rock, Ruler
S – Saviour, Sanctifier, Shepherd, Strong, Sustainer
T – Truth, Tender
U – Unchanging, Upholder, Unbiased, Unflinching, Unfailing,
    Unstoppable
V – Victorious, Vindicator
W – Way, Word, Worthy, Wise, Watchful
X – Xpert (Good at everything)
Y – Yahweh
Z – Zealous

You can create your own list – if you so desire. Just send up
your praise... and break those chains. Your praise has power!

Armed with the Word
The Name of Christ
His Blood and Shield
My Praise is the launching pad

Faith is the force
Prayer is the key
All things are possible
If I only believe.

God has provided
All that I need
His divine power
Gave me everything

I overcome
By the power of the Blood
A new name in place
I'm breaking chains with my praise

Written by Nadine Blair
NADSINK
September 1, 2019 – 5:06pm

Chapter 5

SING YOUR SONG – Trust His Heart; Follow His Lead

How can we sing when we are in a strange land? How can we follow when fear is present? When the unknown is just that – unknown?

If I hear one more word prophesied over me...! It is a lovely thing to be in a setting and a Prophet, Pastor, or Priest calls you up and prays over then gives you a specific word. But harder still to step out in faith on that word.

Often it seems like something insurmountable. And truth be told, many times, for me – it is. But only if I attempt it in my flesh. The practice of seeking the face of God, listening for His next step and His guidance, and stepping out in faith are all well and good. I cry like the man in the Bible – "Lord, I believe; help Thou mine unbelief." Mark 9:24 (KJV)

It is important to remember that if we go on our own, we will never complete or maybe even dare to start the assignment. However, in God, with God, and by God's Grace – we can do all things.

This faith walk though, is easier said than done. It is a struggle that is very real and many who seem to have it all intact, are really struggling on the inside.

Take Moses' story for instance – the inspiration for my song *"Your Presence – Send Me"*.

Moses' very life was filled with many "to-and-fro's".

Watch his journey – God wanted a man for a particular job. By divine order and a series of chaotic circumstances, God placed a baby in a basket in a river – that just happened to lead to Pharaoh's daughter's "outside bathroom". He further planned it that the very mother of the baby would be "hired" – yes, paid – to nurse the baby – her very own baby.

The series of circumstances deepens with a friendship between Moses and the son of Pharaoh. Their friendship was strong – the bond was unique. But all of this was part of a bigger plan. God had placed Moses in the right family – where he would learn their ways and befriend the son of his soon to be biggest challenge, and ultimately favored Moses with lessons he would use on the other side of his journey.

Do you feel as if your life is like that – a series of unexplained, unfortunate, uncanny events? Could there be a greater good at work? Very often we miss the beauty around us because we are so focused on the clouds above us. Moses had no clue that he would be called to lead God's people. He never thought he would be the chosen one to stand before God. With all he had to face, God was still in control, still working His ultimate plan. All Moses had to do was trust, obey, follow, and believe.

Moses began to realize who he was and something inside him would not stand for the mistreatment of his people.

The Scripture tells the story:

Exodus 2:11-15 (KJV):

11 And it came to pass in those days, when Moses was grown, that he went out unto his brethren, and looked on their burdens: and he spied an Egyptian smiting an Hebrew, one of his brethren. 12 And he looked this way and that way, and when he saw that there was no man, he slew the Egyptian, and hid him in the sand. 13 And when he went out the second day, behold, two men of the Hebrews strove together: and he said to him that did the wrong, Wherefore smitest thou thy fellow? 14 And he said, Who made thee a prince and a judge over us? Intendest thou to kill me, as thou killedst the Egyptian? And Moses feared, and said, Surely this thing is known. 15 Now when Pharaoh heard this thing, he sought to slay Moses. But Moses fled from the face of Pharaoh, and dwelt in the land of Midian:

His comfortable life just got ripped apart in a few verses. Moses was now on the run.

This sets the background for a mighty ruler – one we are still talking about today. Movies, books, songs, and more have been written and still are being produced today, telling the story of this man with a lisp and a life full of drama. This is a powerful man. Surely, he must have had it all together – right?

I have heard it all. "Nadine Blair? She's a powerful woman." "Nadine can do anything." And so on. Well, guess what? Nadine does not always have it all together. Surprise!!!! Sometimes before going on stage I am a nervous wreck – I have no clue what I will be saying and wonder if I will be effective. Will I meet the needs of the promoter and keep the energy going all night and, above all, will I please God?

Nerves are real, friends. But Fae Ellington shared once – it is pure adrenalin – just you use that adrenalin and let it work for you.

I don't know that Moses was thinking about adrenalin when God said to him, "Go and let my people go". After all that he had been through, Moses was still the man God wanted to use.

Oh!? So, you thought that because you failed God a million times and ran away from Him and His call, that He is done with you? Wrong! God's purpose is calling you and you will need to get up and run back to God. You will have to go and "let His people go" – that gift God placed in you; that call He placed on your life... is calling you.

Preach that message!
Go to the mission field!
Write that book!
Sing Your Song!

The God of this Universe looks down and says, "Moses, GO!" And Moses pauses and negotiates with God for someone to speak on his behalf. God sends him Aaron.

Sometimes that is all you need. Go before God – Accept the call – Ask for an Aaron. Whatever you do – just DO what God has called you to do. Just "Sing Your Song"!

You know the story – the many plagues, the parting of the Red Sea – now this trumps allllll – What a miracle! Moving over one million persons from one point to the next – without trains, buses, cars. And now with the evidence of God fighting for His people – cloud by day, fire by night... here comes a great body of water in front of them and mountains on the left and right... What now shall we do? I look to You!

Mountains to my left and right
The army of the enemy behind me
Situation seemed impossible
But before me stood a sea of opportunity

Then The Lord made a Way
Where there seemed to be no Way
And A Miracle that only He could do
Unfolded before me

He Made A Water Wall
He Made a Water Wall

Written by Nadine Blair
NADSINK

This song came to me during a Jamaica Youth For Christ Prayer Breakfast as Rev. Stevenson Samuels preached a word about God making a way.

Moses could have chosen to run again – but this time, *this time*, Moses stood his ground and with rod in hand and the Voice of Jehovah – Moses stretched out the rod and BAM!!!! God Made A Water Wall.

It is important to note the two sides of this miracle. God allowed this same water wall to be a way of escape for His people, but it was also a place of destruction for the enemy. Wha God cyaa do? (What is it that God cannot do?)

My God!!!

I want to get to my song for this chapter but boy – the story a sweet mi!

After all of this, God still was not through with Moses. The story continues with more lessons for Moses. He learned management skills. Then there was God's University with Lecturer, Professor Jethro – the class was Management and Communications 101. So many lessons along the way. So many miracles seen first-hand.

Moses has seen God send plagues, part waters, provide daily "manna" for His people, and so much more right there in the desert. And yet is still struggling with believing for himself that God is really with him.

Moses, we know how you felt. Admit it people – there are times when after all God has done, we will want that reminder – that reassurance of His presence, of His directive, of His Will.

Exodus 33 tells of a conversation between Moses and God. (This is how I start the song for this chapter).

◆◆◆

THE PROMISE OF GOD'S PRESENCE

Exodus 33:12-18 King James Version (KJV)

12 And Moses said unto the Lord, See, thou sayest unto me, Bring up this people: and thou hast not let me know whom thou wilt send with me. Yet thou hast said, I know thee by name, and thou hast also found grace in my sight. 13 Now therefore, I pray thee, if I have found grace in thy sight, shew me now thy way, that I may know thee, that I may find grace in thy sight: and consider that this nation is thy people. 14 And he said, My presence shall go with thee, and I will give thee rest. 15 And he said unto him, If thy presence go not with me, carry us not up hence. 16 For wherein shall it be known here that I and thy people have found grace in thy sight? is it not in that thou goest with us? so shall we be separated, I and thy people, from all the people that are upon the face of the earth. 17 And the Lord said unto Moses, I will do this thing also that thou hast spoken: for thou hast found grace in my sight, and I know thee by name. 18 And he said, I beseech thee, shew me thy glory.

This is the premise of the song "Your Presence – Send Me".

We were on our way to minister in the Cayman Islands. Perpetual Praise has had quite a few memorable ministry trips there. We have seen the power of God move in such a mighty way.

As we prepared for one of those trips, we met for prayer and it came just like that – flowing like a river. We were holding hands and in the middle of the prayer I had to let go and begin to write.

This is what I heard:

Verse 1
And I, I will not go, lest Your presence is with me
Show me Your favor, Lord
I, I'll only do what You want me to do
And I, can only say what You want me to say
Lord, have Your way

Chorus 1
So speak, So guide
So lead – Walk by my side

Chorus 2
I'll go – I'll say – I'll do –
Have Your way
I'll go – I'll say – I'll do
As long as Your presence is with me

Verse 2
Lord I want to see Your Glory
Your goodness and mercy
Every day of my life
And I, I want You to hide me in the cleft of the Rock
Lord, I believe that in Your hands I am safe

Chorus 1
So speak, So guide
So lead – Walk by my side

Chorus 2
I'll go – I'll say
I'll do – Have Your way
I'll go – I'll say
I'll do

As long as Your presence is with me

Bridge
If Your presence is with me
Then the whole world will see
Let them know You sent me
I'll go
I'll do
I'll say – yes!
I'll go
I'll do
I'll say – yes!
Just have Your way, Lord!

Written by Nadine Blair

Thanks to Jermaine Edwards, Latoya HD and iWorshipp singers and band who helped me record this song. Feeling blessed to have had Rhoda Isabella and Alicia Taylor (nee Foster) singing on my song... awesomeness.

I encourage you as I encourage myself in the Lord. God wants to use you. Broken, beaten, battered, bruised – He still sees value in you.

Disobedient? Run back to the place of instruction and GO!

Despondent? Don't give up! He still sees you – the real you.

Desperate? He will do whatever needs to be done to get you

out of that situation. Part the waters and drown the enemy.

He will be found if He is wholeheartedly sought
He will calm the troubled places in your heart
Purpose will guide you to where you belong
So write that book – SING YOUR SONG!

Written by Nadine Blair
NADSINK
September 7, 2019 9:14am

Chapter 6
SING YOUR SONG – Happiness is a State of Mind

The mind is a powerful thing. I was sharing with one of my team members recently that sometimes what is real in our minds is not so in reality. She shared how when she walked into a particular gathering, she noticed eyes looking at her. She kept wondering, "Why is everybody looking at me? They don't want me to be here?"

I shared that everyone will have those moments where it seems as if everyone IS in fact looking at you. But what they are thinking may be something totally opposite to what we have "conjured" up in our minds.

They may be saying "Wow! She is so pretty," "I want to be like her," and so on. In her case, I told her that they may even be saying, "She is a browning and pretty like wah" – I had to laugh.

I have been there. And it took me awhile to get to a place of self-acceptance. The saying that shows that it really should not matter to you what people are saying about you – is true. Don't make it matter… But I add to it –

What people think or say about you
Should never become your focus
Evaluate what has been said
And work on what is needed the most
Throw away the negative
Learn from any mistake

What people think or say about you
Can make or break your day.
How you respond is the key
So manage you and let them be!

Written by Nadine Blair
NADSINK
September 7, 2019 – 9:31am

I have heard my parents mention in messages – "The Heart of the Matter is the Matter of the Heart."

At the center of it all is this – what is in your heart? For out of it will come a smile or frown.

Your heart; your mind; your soul – for the purpose of this discussion – is all the same.

Happiness comes from the Lord. It is learning to be content no matter the state. It is focusing on what you want – the mind – and not on what you see, for what you see and hear around you may really not be positive. But what you allow to move you and to drive you must be founded in something bigger than yourself. This, my friend, is how persons can have a smile on their face while facing the most difficult situations.

I wanted to write a happy song. Jehovah God has been that place of safety, that peace in the midst of turmoil – and yes – I, Nadine Blair, have seen some days when I feel so alone – so torn and hurt by some persons so close to me.

How can someone you invited into your own home... probably even shared a bed and broke bread with... be so heartless? How can friends take pleasure in your downfall? Tears fill my eyes even now as I write, but then I remember what the Lord has done and I smile again.

It is so true that when I am weak and I take the time to call on the Lord – He does answer. It may not be in the way I want Him to or in the timing I desired Him to, but He remembers me – and over and over again He has been my stay.

◆◆◆

PRAY, NADINE, PRAY!

The good old hymn said it so well – What A Friend We Have in Jesus by <u>Joseph M. Scriven</u>, 1855. In it he suggests that we go through pain because we forget to remember to pray about the issues we face. Recently, I would be awakened with these words ringing in my head: "Pray, Nadine, pray!"

To be honest, there were mornings I just stayed in the bed and whispered two lines and went back to sleep. But there were those times I would get up (fewer than I want to admit) and walk the floor of my house and do just that... PRAY!

During the summer of 2017 there were a few nights I was awakened by a pain, a feeling, a sense of a storm brewing – something was happening. It was not pain like a headache, but a very deep sense that someone, somewhere was fighting against me.

What did I do? What do YOU do when faced with those times of dismal, darkening, desperate, deafening pain?

Well, I did what I do best. I worshipped. What should you do? SING YOUR SONG! Find a praise in your belly and worship.

Sometimes there will be more questions than answers. Sometimes the wait will be longer than you anticipated. But don't focus on the negative. You must look at it; take what you can from it; learn the lessons, and keep moving; keep smiling; keep praising; keep singing.

In Philippians 4:12, Paul talked about deciding that whatever state of mind he was in he was resolute and steadfast in spirit that he would be content.

We also have to learn when to speak – and if we really need to. Sometimes people just need their space to work through things in their mind and after that they are ready to go again. Then it is time to talk.

Recently, an event brought pain on so many levels. It would have been easy to walk away thinking bad about some persons. Why would they do such a thing? Or say such a thing?

I had to pull up my socks and pray continuously for each person affected and when the time allowed, I made a few calls. It was eye-opening. What I was thinking, what people were saying – was far from what really happened. And on the flip side, what they were thinking that I did, was far from the truth.

Had I not taken the time to call and talk it out, we could have been left walking through our days thinking badly of someone when the scene in our minds was not real.

There are situations that have at the core the power to split families and break down years of friendship in one single blow.

Always pray for your enemies and frenemies. Keep your heart pure. And always, always remember – what is real in my mind may be a misguided missile of destruction sent from the enemy to separate us.

Let your first thought be love. And fill your heart and mind and soul with thoughts, songs, hymns, and messages of love.

This is how you overcome. Keep reading the Word of God and ask the Holy Spirit to help you differentiate what is real and what is imagined.

If you can find your praise in the middle of your storm;
If you will let the Word of God – your response – inform;
If you will allow the Holy Spirit, the turmoil calm
You will find the strength and will to go on.

Written by Nadine Blair
NADSINK

I've often said it is better to respond than react. A reaction suggests no processing of thought. There is, however, a place for reaction – it can still be immediate and intentional because of what is in your heart. Think of a rebuke. A covering under the blood of Jesus.

But in cases of disagreement and not seeing eye to eye, we ought to pause and allow time to go work through our thoughts and possible responses; evaluate the situation, and allow the Holy Spirit to guide our response.

The joy that follows, the peace that reigns after – will be rooted and grounded in something bigger than the very argument or disagreement.

◆◆◆
SINGING YOUR SONG

This was probably the first "real" song I wrote and it was a time when the world was singing "Don't Worry – Be Happy". I wanted to give the world ... OK, *my* world, something happy to sing about.

SINGING YOUR SONG

CHORUS
Oh Lord, when I'm weak You make me strong

You keep me going on
And now You've got me singing Your song
And I, I could not repay
You release me from the chains
And now You've got me praising Your name

VERSE 1

Never knew the day would come
When I would smile again
Sin had control of me
Losing was my game
With love and tenderness
You gently took me in

Now I'm standing on The Rock
Winner is my name

BRIDGE 1

I was searching for You – All my life long
Longing for You – Emptiness gone

Wondering just – How could I go on
Till You came along – Now I'm singing Your song
Loving You – One hundred percent
Praising You – I'll never let it end
Living for You – Ain't gonna stop
Even when I drop – I'm gonna get up – get up back

CHORUS

BRIDGE 2

You're a mighty God! You're a mighty God!
You're a mighty God! Mighty good God!

VAMP

So when I'm sad – I praise!
When I'm sick – I praise!
No job – I praise, I praise, I praise!
All alone – I praise!
Friends are gone – I praise!
Can't go on – I praise, I praise, I praise!

You lift me up – I praise!
You fill my cup – I praise!
You give me joy – I praise, I praise, I praise!
I lift my hands to You – I praise!
I lift my voice in praise – I praise!
I have no choice – I praise, I praise, I praise!

BRIDGE 2

You're a mighty God! You're a mighty God!
You're a mighty God! Mighty Good God!

CHORUS

Oh Lord, when I'm weak
You make me strong
You keep me going on
And now You've got me singing Your song
And I, I could not repay
You release me from the chains
And now You've got me praising Your name

Written by Nadine Blair (years ago...)

Thanks to Johnny Clarke and all the fine musicians and singers who helped to make this recording happen. I am forever grateful.

When we are weak and only limited to what our eyes can see,

our Jehovah God will show up if we open our hearts to Him.

Such a confirmation – for right now as I type, I am hearing the instrumental for this song done by Karl Gibson on bass, being played on the radio. I love it when God does that.

Allow yourself to be happy. This comes from constant, repetitive meeting times with God – alone in His presence, allowing Him to heal the hurts.

My parents tell of a true story of a Church of God missionary who was locked up for his faith. (We are a part of the New Testament Church of God with World Offices in Cleveland, Tennessee – the group is known as the Church of God Worldwide but adopted the name "New Testament Church of God" in a few countries where the name "Church of God" was already being used.)

This missionary was assigned to one of the countries in the 10/40 Window. This refers to regions of the eastern hemisphere located between 10 and 40 degrees north of the equator with the least access to the gospel of Christ.

He was locked up for trying to spread the gospel and his duty as a prisoner was to grind the mess – effluent – waste... with his bare feet.

When he was locked up the church in the rest of the world was called to pray. And as word of his crisis spread, more prayers were going up. And the prayers availed much in the end – thanks be to God.

But wait – let me go back to this man in the "dung-filled" container walking around daily, crushing the mess with his bare feet.

This man of God could have gone mad, angry, crazy,

miserable. But the most powerful of stories was to be revealed when he was returned to his country. In those times when he walked through the mess, he chose not to focus on what he was seeing… or smelling, for that matter!

This missionary sang his song. As he walked, he began to sing...

I come to the garden alone
While the dew is still on the roses[3]

How can you possibly be singing such a song while walking around in a pile of dung?

His happiness – his peace of mind – his joy –was founded in something and someone deeper than that which his physical situation allowed him to be in.

His state of mind was beyond what those prison guards could comprehend.

CHORUS

And He walks with me and He talks with me
And He tells me I am His own
And the joy we share as we tarry there
None other has ever known
C. Austin Miles – 1912

And watch how God works... we may not know the story behind what spurred this song by C Austin Miles in 1912, but the power of the song stayed alive - long enough to encourage this missionary years later - and further the many who have heard this testimony and are still alive today encouraging me

---

[3] "In the Garden" by C. Austin Miles. Public Domain.

as I write and even now as you read this story.

Every time I hear this testimony, I am encouraged and I pray you have been too.

What is this mountain you are facing?
What is this trial so strong?
There is One greater than any Goliath
Find your center in Christ and
SING YOUR SONG!
Real joy and genuine happiness
Is built on Jehovah God
Let Him be your reason for singing

Let Christ be the theme of Your song.

Written by Nadine Blair
NADSINK

Chapter 7
SING YOUR SONG – When There Is Nothing Else You Can Do – Literally!

Recently on a flight back from New York, I encountered something frighteningly scary yet beautifully orchestrated.

The weekend was packed. I left Jamaica on Thursday evening and after a long flight and the kindness of strangers who became my hosts and driver (Thank you Francine and Joshua), I shared in a broadcast on Friday that featured Carlene Davis' new short remix project from her latest full album, *The Assignment*. And what an assignment I had that weekend.

On Saturday I had the joy of performing emcee duties for Fun In The Son, Bronx, New York. (I pause to send up prayers for the many in New York, who have been affected by the horrible virus. May you find strength during this very hard time.)

The "give back to the community" event started midday and ran to just about midnight – surely a long, hard day, but I was pumped and worshipped all day and night. Who wouldn't with ministry from power houses like Glacia Robinson, Carlene Davis-Cowan, Papa San, and Eddie James? I sing "Breakthrough" like an anthem here in Jamaica. *"You are the God of the Breakthrough"* – **Eddie James** I can't thank you enough for that song.

I was so, extremely, blessed. After one hour of well-needed

sleep, it was off to the airport to catch the early morning flight back to Jamaica.

What was ahead could not have been expected.

The flight was good. I slept some and was preparing my mind as well for another time of ministry as emcee that Sunday night at Denbigh Gospel Showcase.

Sometime during the flight, I sensed The Lord wanting me to worship. Between tired eyes and mind and a hungry belly, I mumbled a few "Praise the Lord," "Thank You Jesus," and more. I thought about His love and goodness and worshipped quietly in my heart.

It was about time to land and all of a sudden it started.

My first-time ever flying was a trip to Nassau, Bahamas. Even now I pause to pray for those who lost everything and more – yes more – during Hurricane Dorian in 2019. May you know we are praying AND doing... we love you.

On that trip I encountered my first time flying through clouds. No one told me about this. Those lovely, soft-looking, cotton-like things in the sky can cause such a "shake". The plane started vibrating – well, that's what it felt like. And I quickly drew for my "Testament" – yes, those little New Testament Bibles with Psalms and Proverbs at the back. And I read softly but really trying to assure myself that all would be well...

The Lord is my Shepherd
I shall not want...

Well I survived that flight – and it would be the first of many. Thanks be to God for His protection every single time.

After years of flying hither and thither – my longest direct flight being from Kingston to London on BWIA – and several trips to and from Cleveland, Tennessee to attend then Lee College (now Lee University – Go Flames!!!) I had never experienced what I did on that day.

Carlene Davis and her backup singer were on that flight as well and later told me that the plane had actually circled about three times – apparently, we could not land.

The plane suddenly dipped and rocked and sped up and slowed down and dipped and rocked and... you get the picture. The only thing we did not do was hit a reverse in the sky – lol.

From the back of the plane I heard, "Jesus please remember us!" In the middle of the plane a man cried out, "Jehovah God – we cry out to You for help!" Beside me was a woman crying out the name of "Jesus!" and at the front of the plane was another lady crying out to God.

It was a beautiful sound of chaotic yet beautifully orchestrated praise and cries for help. The lady beside me was now jolted from her calm demeanor, which she had tried to maintain all through the flight. I wondered how she remained so calm.

Whenever we travel, we ought to be aware that there are persons who are flying with ulterior motives in life. Some of us choose to worship Jehovah God and others worship the dark enemy. Always be on alert. Always pray. Always cover yourself.

I don't know if anyone like that was on board, but I do know the power of our prayer, the results of our praise, and the outcome when we sing our song to Jehovah God.

I sat there worshipping in silence. I didn't know if I was happy to trust God more than I was glad for the outward display of worship that burst out in the plane. It did not matter the class of person – and I say that knowing we are all equal in the sight of Christ. It did not matter the upbringing, the money in the bank, nor the stories behind the stories, we were in a situation that levelled everyone. First class or other class was all one. And we had a choice – the only choice – to call on the NAME OF THE LORD JESUS CHRIST – SON OF THE LIVING GOD.

In my heart, as I worshipped, I heard ...

"…Underneath are the everlasting arms…" Deuteronomy 33:27 KJV

It was a one-line "song" that kept ringing over in my head.

The man on my right was silent. I think inside he was screaming – that's what I think – and maybe just trying to be strong. The woman in the row across from him may have been his family member or friend – they were travelling together and she was calling on the name of the Lord. Calling on Jesus. Calling for help.

When we finally landed, she said to him that he should thank God. It seemed he did not agree but obliged and finally, after a little prodding, said, "Thank You Jesus."

The elderly man in the middle of plane kept on thanking God – he was loud and I loved it. Praise God yaaa. Because many there are in another situation with a different tale to tell – some don't make it to tell the tale themselves. This story could have had a different ending.

'The Eternal God is your refuge

*And underneath are the everlasting arms.' Deuteronomy
33:27 KJV*

A song is now being birthed from this and I can't wait to sing it. But until then I invite you to remember this verse when you travel. Pray and cover yourself, your family, everything that concerns you. And trust Him – whether walking across the street, driving in your car, bus or train, flying, or in a ship.... Underneath are the everlasting arms of Jehovah God.

His love for you will keep you.
His wisdom will be your guide
Jehovah God is a shelter safe
His angels - above and beside.

Written by Nadine Blair
NADSINK

Chapter 8
SING YOUR SONG – And Change the World

The ideology behind these three words is many-fold.

Sing Your Song was birthed from an encouragement to us from fellow musician, Noel Robinson, to not be so anxious to do covers of another person's music. There are times when this can be done and bring a fresh approach to a song.

However, Noel really wanted us to sing OUR songs. To write our own songs and present them to the world. No matter how small or large that stage.

He was encouraging us to recognize and awaken the talent in us.

He also wanted us to do OUR reggae worship, reggae gospel. Whatever it is the Lord has given us.

I had an experience years ago that never left me. I was still "fresh" at Lee College and went on a trip. I think it was with a choir – or maybe a group, but we were on a bus and we had stopped on the way. I don't remember if I was playing the music or singing it as back then we didn't have cell phones and such like.

But the American friends heard something and were asking me for gospel reggae.

Back then the fight to sing and worship in reggae was so fierce. We were doing better than the days when the great

Claudelle Clarke was told she could not sing her songs with all of that music and jing-bang. Or when Insights Gospel Band was "stoned" (with orange juice boxes) at Stephanie Hall – because Jamaicans were just not ready for reggae gospel – or our homeland type of music – in gospel.

So here I am in mid-USA and white American Christian young people were begging me for gospel reggae – this thing that at the time at home in J.A. was being frowned upon.

I think it would have been a cassette player but it was for sure the Grace Thrillers that I was playing. And they loved it.

I asked them about country gospel.

At that time, and still today, Jamaicans absolutely loved and embraced country gospel... yah hear! (said with a southern accent)

When I shared that, they were aghast. They would have none of it. To them they equated country gospel with the secular country songs... so whenever they heard a country gospel song – they are thinking about the "other" non-Christian country songs. And then it dawned on me.... Mark 6:4 (NKJV)

⁴ But Jesus said to them, "A prophet is not without honor except in his own country, among his own relatives, and in his own house."

Our own Jamaicans probably do the same thing. Some of them anyways. When they hear the gospel in the reggae genre it reminds them too much of the secular – un-Christian music and rather than focus on the message – the words – the spirit in which it was birthed, they are focusing on the genre – the beat – what they remember of the secular songs.

This is what these young people in mid to south Tennessee were doing. They were hearing and focusing not on the message, the words, nor the spirit the gospel country songs are written in, but on the genre. It struck a nerve in them.

This lesson has never left me.

And unfortunately, there are some who still today focus on the genre – the type of music – and not on the message. And to each his own. My takeaway – we never know what is in the heart of a man – let God be the final Judge.

In Chapter One I told you about Noel and him just sharing and saying SING YOUR SONG.

I continue to encourage you to sing what God has given you; your own original songs. But he was also saying sing your genre – because the world is waiting to hear it – the world is accepting of and waiting for gospel worship in the genre of reggae and that is our own Jamaican made stuff.

When Noel said those words – I also heard and received it as saying – do what God has called you to do.

Write that book. I have waited for so long until my "song" became "wait just a little longer" = procrastination. I got so busy with life that I had little time to write. I also allowed fear and a bunch of what-ifs to take over my mind. What if people don't buy the book? What if they don't like it? Yes, me – the 'great' Nadine Blair.

Pray, Nadine, pray.

Sing, Nadine, sing

Write, Nadine, write

Put your name there and whatever it is that you have sensed that God is trusting you with – say it and get up and do it. Time waits on no man.

Start your business! Plan your retreats and conferences! Do that Jamaica and Caribbean tour! Just GO! (As soon as the challenge with this virus is over that is)

Sing Your Song also means no matter the darkness, no matter the fears – find your hope and strength in Jehovah God and do that thing. Worship when you don't know what to do. Praise when you feel like giving up. Bless the name of the Lord whether you feel like it or not.

Sing Your Song unto the Lord.

I have always written poems. When I was in high school (Immaculate Conception High School) my fellow classmates would ask me all the time to write poems for them. They would use these poems to encourage others or give to their boyfriends – lol – now if you are a guy who had a girlfriend attending Immaculate in the late 80's and you received a poem from her – it may have been written by me. (It is an all-girls school)

A lot of things stopped me from publishing a book of poems. I sent a manuscript of my poems to England years ago and what I got back was not encouraging so I just left it. Every now and again, however, I wonder if I would one day find a published book with my poems and link it back to that person or place that I sent those poems. Wishful thinking – but I would be well rich. I still have the old manuscripts with my notes and everything.

Your platform – your world – may not be as big as mine. HOLD ON – and I know that my platform is definitely not as big as so many great people out there too. But this I know: that God has called each of us for a purpose and this purpose must be fulfilled. Rondell Positive says it – "My purpose a call mi – and a time fi mi answer!" (My purpose is calling me. And it is time that I answer) God is not only a hiding place and strength in time of weakness – and so much more. God is strategic. He had each of us born in this time for a particular purpose. I could not have been born any other time. My assignment is linked to this era.

While I am still breathing – while I am still here – let my mission always be – to do the will of my Father – To follow in His Will – Fulfill my purpose – To SING MY SONG!

Chapter 9

SING YOUR SONG – You Were Made for This!

I am aware that life seems to be passing by me so very fast. Everybody else seems to be writing their books, planning their conferences, doing their tours, making their albums, and I feel like I am sitting on a fence watching – waiting for what? I don't know.

I am all too aware as well that persons may be saying, "Nadine naaa do nutn" (Nadine isn't doing anything). My semi-comfort comes in knowing that I have just about done it all. I have held several conferences over a five-year period; I have done my form of encouraging and recognizing the powerful talents that are here in Jamaica – super-proud of my Jamaican gospel artistes; I have done some recordings of songs and led a myriad of worship sessions across the island and overseas.

At my 50th birthday celebration, I celebrated 50 years of age; 25 years in radio and 40 years in gospel music. But truth be told, deep down I am very aware that there is so much more that I can do.

I have always loved talking with and encouraging young people. I remember a powerful testimony shared with me by the founder of Passion and Purity – a move to empower young people across the island to be their best selves IN CHRIST. Donnette Norman is the gem. She along with her husband birthed and have seen this move through over many years.

My group and I visit schools every year, and this is one of my high points: to sing, to usher them into the presence of God, and to pray for them.

One year, we were invited to come back to a school for the close of the year – separate from the regular ISCF (Inter School Christian Fellowship) meetings. We got there and the normally full auditorium was basically empty. GT Sounds was set up and my skeletal team and I walked in to minister. We sang like we were singing to a packed stadium. Worship was rich.

That day my group was limited to two male singers, a three-part band, and me. Soon, even some of the band members started singing. It was just God...

The altar call came and I called everyone up to the altar. I came off the stage and went to share from the heart to these faithful few that had gathered.

I held their faces, one by one, called them by name and spoke into their lives. Tears flowed. Worship grew. Some finally surrendered to God and others recommitted their lives to Christ. It was amazing. The few of us never made a difference in our output and the outcome was for the glory of God. Souls were won to the kingdom.

Weeks later, I got a text from Miss Norman. A newspaper article showed an interview with one of the students. She mentioned that date – when the hall was empty – when the altar was full of the few that gathered but also when she and others surrendered to Jesus Christ.

Tears filled my eyes as I read.

You see, some may see a small audience as a discouragement. But as I always teach my team members in Perpetual Sounds of Praise, don't let that stop you from ministering and giving your best.

Donnette further mentioned that they were not just saved but that they were *"On Fire for God"*!

The time of ministry in the most unexpected of circumstances brought forth powerful, anointed young people who – we never know – may just change the world.

I was indeed made for this... called for this... and I am humbled that God would see me fit to be used.

TO GOD BE THE GLORY!

In the Fall of 2019, I had the urge to hit the road... go into schools – not wait for the regular ISCF concerts but just GO! And meet with youths in an intimate setting – up close and personal.

I never stalled. After a few calls – the calendar started to unravel and I was visiting several schools throughout the semester.

To be honest, maybe two of those experiences had me questioning myself. The students just sat there. I was not sure if they were hearing me – if they found what I was saying interesting – but I stood in the comfort of knowing that I believed with all my heart God told me to do it and I just DID IT. I "sang my song".

My heart was touched. I got comments and reports and I felt like God was pleased.

Here is what God told me to share: I sat at the computer after hearing the lead and said, "God what do you want me to say to these young people?"

I heard, "YOU WERE MADE FOR THIS"

And I began to write...

YOU WERE MADE FOR THIS

Carved out in your DNA is the word VICTORIOUS
Hidden with Christ – The Holy Spirit abides in us
Daughter of the Most High
Son of Adonai
YOU WERE MADE FOR THIS

So don't be taken aback when the world wants you to follow
Don't be too timid to speak up
Nor God's name in public Hallow
Be the first to rep Christ
Act nice
To His Word Subscribe
From the wages of sin
Think twice
It's appointed unto man
Not to die twice
But once and then it's done
What valuable lessons have you garnered from
The valuable moments in His presence sought
Oh wait
Have you even taken the time?
Then how do you plan to live above the tide?
YOU WERE MADE FOR THIS

Inside of you is a hidden secret
One the enemy knows and wants to hide you from it
Learn what it is and you can change nations
Shun where you find it and you will live on rations
Ask God for the insight
The foresight
The might
To stand when tempted

To lef wrong and do right
To be the odd one
Sitting on the sidelines
As long as YOU know
You are seated with Christ

So what am I saying…

I'm saying there is more in you
I'm saying there is gold in you
And the minors will major in disqualifying you

If you just nonchalantly dispossess
Your possession
Yes – it's already in you
Don't you forget it

It's what David sought after
What Saul threw after
What Daniel risked all for
What lions lost appetite for
It is gold
It is power
It is Christ in you the hope for every hour
You face – You face with Christ
You are not alone
When you walk like lions

There is more inside of you
And You were made for this
The word says you are already victorious
The battle that you face now
You already won it
Flash could tell you if he was even really on this planet
Hulk, superman, ain't got nothing on this

You were made for this
Now supersize THIS!

You were made with faith enough to move a mountain
Small as a seed – you can overcome the problem

You were made with a sound deep inside
Did you know that Jesus hears every single cry...
You make today – Or did last week
He already has the answers to next year's questions you will
seek

And for all the tears you have and will cry
God bottles them up – You're the apple of His eye
You were made for this
You have what it takes
You are not alone – You are not a mistake

Center your thoughts
Will your emotion
Let Christ steer your ship
In this raging ocean
You are stronger than you know
Wiser than what you show
Smarter than you think
YOU WERE MADE FOR THIS!

Written by Nadine Blair
NADSINK
SEPTEMBER 24, 2019 - 8:10PM

Now we walk through each letter
M-A-D-E F-O-R T-H-I-S!
Hope it makes it easy for you to remember.

MANAGE what tries to manage you

- ∂ We will always be faced with challenges. Whether we react or respond will determine the picture of our lives that will be painted.
- ∂ To react suggests lack of thought – no processing of consequences
- ∂ As against responding which usually means the listener has had time to think it through. Is this true? Fully true or partly so? Learn to take out what applies to you and cast the rest to the wind.
- ∂ You will learn as you get older that somethings are not worth spending time – wasting sweat over.
- ∂ You will learn – as I learnt over time and am still learning – that somethings are best left alone. We cannot always win a battle and we cannot always win in convincing persons to see our point of view. Remember we are each on our own journey. Another person may not have learnt a lesson you already learnt that taught you how to react to a particular situation. Give them time…and don't allow it to eat at you.

Learn this simple truth that it really boils down to how you look at the problem which is really the problem. Those who win are those who see problems as stepping stones and are always ready to learn a lesson and move on.

Don't let it manage you. Manage that stressor.

APPLY what you learn – don't waste it

- ∂ This was prepared for secondary school students – high schoolers. But this point can be applied to all age groups - Use your time to learn all you can.
- ∂ Focus on learning – studying – appropriating time for Study above all else. We should never feel that learning should end but rather always be open to see what else is there to learn.
- ∂ Guess what? There will still be time for everything else. Some schoolers feel cheated of their time. But each stage in life has its purpose and plays an important role in helping us become the best we can be. Don't miss the lessons in each stage.
- ∂ And don't say you won't need it all

I studied French at Immaculate Conception High School and I did another year at Lee College (now University – in Cleveland, Tennessee). I chose French because it just sounded so good. And besides they called it the "romantic language".

There were times I wondered when would I really use French. Until my trip to Europe.

Lee College started a new feature called "Semester in Europe" and I was chosen to be among the first students to spend 13 weeks in England. It was amazing.

One memorable incident is one where I got to help someone who spoke French. We stayed at the YMCA and it was back when cell phones were not in yet and pay phones were the main point of contact in places like those.

I was passing the front office and overheard what seemed like a woman in distress, trying to communicate with the person on the phone.

Another thing about payphones is that if you were calling

outside of the country, you needed the assistance of an operator. She was obviously trying to express herself to the operator and her message was just not going through. She was speaking French.

Well I jumped in. I spoke what French I could to let her know I would be happy to help her, took the phone and became an instant interpreter. I was able to assist the young lady and she got to connect with whomever she was trying to reach in France.

My how many years of studying, remembering and learning "francais" paid off after all. Now I don't know what the urgency of the call was about, but I have never forgotten that incident. Had I been in her shoe, I would be so grateful and I can imagine that was how she felt.

Je ne sais pas ce qui s'est passé, mais j'ai été heureux de vous aider (I don't know what happened, but I was happy to help!)

 ∂ Focus on making your time in school all about garnering all the knowledge you can – you will be better than you already think or imagine you are

DON'T SETTLE – not everything that glitters is gold

 ∂ I was so convinced he was the right person – he knew the word, he went to church, he had great plans for his life.
 ∂ I chose to listen with my eyes and not my head. I chose to settle. See my next book for a little peek into that story. Just be sure you are in God's will and purpose for your life.
 ∂ Don't settle – wait on God and let Him choose for you

> ∂ Make that a mantra for everything you do – Don't settle for the job you feel safe in; don't settle for people talking down to you – of course you have already learnt not to react but to respond.

EVALUATE your choices – **EARN** respect

> ∂ It was the silent party everyone wanted to attend but did not really know when it was held and where. I finally got invited one year and on arrival was surprised out of my shoes. There was drinking and dancing. Dancing wasn't my problem per se…but it was not gospel music. And I was not having any of it.

I sat and cried the entire night as friends begged me to participate. "It's just a little fun" "Come and dance with us" – and so on. I wanted to go home.

I share more on this in my next book as well.

The take away however was that the following week, I was greeted by persons who said that they respected me for standing up for what I believed in. It was hard. I was the odd one. I did not want to hurt them nor let them down. But I evaluated my choices and chose not to participate. It was against everything I believed in.

I was alone in my decision. I was alone on the bench crying my eyes out saying that I wanted to leave. But I earned their respect and that was most important. I love them all to this day…but at that time I had to be the odd one – and as alone as I was, I learnt then that it is ok to be the odd one.

Make God proud.

∂ You don't have to follow the crowd – let them follow you as you follow Christ.

FORGE strong and safe friendships and **FIND** sound mentors

∂ Have a crew who are solid, sane and sold out for Christ friends who you can trust to call you out if they see you doing something wrong; You need people in your life.

∂ Mentors – older persons who have been there. The stories may be slightly different but the lessons are never far from the same.

∂ The sooner you learn that you don't know it all - the better.

ORGANIZE – it's a skill that you learn

∂ Start from now to do what you can to be organized. Write down the things you have to do – homework, tasks etc and check them off as you go along.

∂ Learn how to save – DO NOT GET A CREDIT CARD unless you are in a position to pay it off at the end of the month – or at least pay a substantial amount each month. It is better to get a Visa Debit Card where you must have the cash in your account before you spend. Organize your financial life…you will save yourself from a lot of debt pain in the future. Trust me.

∂ Start from now – join a credit union, start a savings plan – don't think that too little is too little.

∂ If I started saving from mi likkle teenie weenie and a grow I would be a millionaire now.

REMOVE NEGATIVE energies

- ∂ Your circumstances don't define you
- ∂ Where you live – where you are in life now – is not the end of your story – good or bad
- ∂ Always look up – look up to God – look up above the problems
- ∂ Joseph had dreams – if he got focused on the "why did my brothers dump me then sell me – why am I in prison – why did the cup bearer forget me – why did Pharaoh's wife do this – why – why – why – and biggest one yet – why did God show me this dream and look where I am. Joseph could have chosen to focus on the negative. He had a lot. But he never gave up on God.
- ∂ Remove negative thoughts – don't entertain them
- ∂ Watch how Jesus rolled when he was going to raise the daughter from the dead. Mark 5 tells the story. Jesus had no time for negativity.

Mark 5:39-42 King James Version (KJV)

39 And when he was come in, he saith unto them, Why make ye this ado, and weep? the damsel is not dead, but sleepeth.

40 And they laughed him to scorn. But when he had put them all out, he taketh the father and the mother of the damsel, and them that were with him, and entereth in where the damsel was lying.

41 And he took the damsel by the hand, and said unto her, Talitha cumi; which is, being interpreted, Damsel, I say unto thee, arise.

42 And straightway the damsel arose, and walked; for she was of the age of twelve years. And they were astonished with a great astonishment.

Remove the negative thoughts, negative energy, negative people from your life. Feast on God's word and know your worth.

TAKE TIME TO KNOW GOD –

- ∂ Take the time to spend time alone with God. You will only grow and be better off in every aspect of your life.
- ∂ He wants that time with you. It is strange how life can fill our space so easily. The tasks at work, at home, at school, at …everywhere. Well at the time of writing this chapter, the pandemic is on and we are forced to stay home and this lends itself to spending more time in prayer.

I am grateful for the time to shut in. Grateful for the "wake up call" to prepare for the rapture – no matter how near or far that will be. Prayerful for those who have lost loved ones and those who have to be on the frontline.

I am thrilled to be convicted over and over by the powerful ministry of Apostle Joshua Selman. You ought to check out his messages on YouTube. #Powerful I tell you. In one of his messages he shared that the key to getting God's attention is not so much rolling on the ground or crying before Him. Apostle Selman shared that our lives must align to the "Kingdom of God coming in the earth". Take time to Know God – For Yourself!!!

He will talk with you – ONE TO ONE

HIDE THE WORD IN YOUR HEART

   ∂   Memorize His word – if your memory nuh suh hot – just read the word. When the time is right – The Holy Spirit will bring back to your memory what you need.

INSPIRE SOMEONE ON YOUR JOURNEY

   ∂   Don't be selfish – pull someone up – a smile – be kind – be patient with people

   ∂   Everyone – each of us – are cultured differently – what we learn at home – how we respond to people and situations will vary because of what we saw our parents do – or picked up from the community – so don't be hasty to judge – take the time to stop and tell someone something nice

   ∂   Suicide is a real fight for many - the new thing now of vaping – where people are trying all sorts of things to get a high and now the challenge of this virus.

Which is worse? Facing the virus or facing the fear. God of Heaven. Help us remember that Your name is higher than any pandemic and higher than fear. I just heard a friend say she was alone and at home and she is fearful. We are in a family chat and everyone started to encourage her.

Call someone. Send a text or voice note and Inspire someone today.

I got a nudge to call or send a voice note to various persons in the Jamaican Gospel Music Network. I love my Jamaican Gospel Artistes and am so collectively proud of them and sent individual notes of encouragement.

You do that with persons close to you today.

Inspire away.

SAVE THE BEST FOR LATER – LITERALLY

   ∂ Sex is great but it can wait.

Live the best that you can in every now that you get! Let God be very pleased with your thoughts, actions and words.

Yes my friend. You were MADE FOR THIS. Someone asked me "What is THIS?" This is that which you were made for. "This" is that mountain you are now facing. "This" is that trial that seems too much. "This" is that test that seems just too hard. God will not give you more than you can bear. You were made for this…and as the word of God says - Everything that goes into a life of pleasing God has been miraculously given to us by getting to know, personally and intimately, the One who invited us to God." MSG 2 Peter 1:3 or as NIV puts it "His divine power has given us everything we need for a godly life through our knowledge of him who called us by his own glory and goodness."

So the next time you face a "this" – remember "that"! You've got this…because He, The Mighty God, has you.

MANAGE what tries to manage you

APPLY what you learn – don't waste it

DON'T SETTLE – not everything that glitters is gold

EVALUATE your choices – **EARN** respect

FORGE strong and safe friendships and **FIND** sound mentors

ORGANIZE – it's a skill that you learn

REMOVE Negative energies

TAKE time to know God

HIDE The Word in your heart

INSPIRE someone on your journey

SAVE the best for last – Sex can wait!

Chapter 10
SING YOUR SONG – Singing Life Through A Valley of Death

The year 2020 started with hopes and visions plenty. Everyone was finding ways to do the regular rhyme with the year slogan. 2020 – The year of Plenty Plenty! Or there was the 2020 – Everything Double Double! Or "We now have 20/20 Vision in 2020".

It started with a high. As does every new year – the sense of newness; I can start again! You feel it. You know it. Every new year is a new page – a new chapter…maybe even a new book. But there was something extra special about the start of 2020.

We made our resolutions; said our prayers and started to travel through the year as it unfolded – one day, one week, one month at a time. Everything was just about normal. We started the diets – and forgot about the diets. We started the diary – and some continued – others of us…well just can't find the diary. We were back to normal days of sorry and sad news headlines and scrambling to make ends meet.

Then like a scene out of a very bad movie – the news of a story that actually started in 2019 – seemed to escalate to unmanaged, unthinkable, unreal scenes. Only these were not just "scenarios" – it was happening. In our world.

Corona Virus had arrived in all its fury.

The first case was actually reported in November 2019…hence the name COVID19 – The Corona Virus

Disease of 2019 had made its way into 2020 and what we thought was only limited to a country, miles away, was somehow coming too close to home.

The World Health Organization declared COVID-19 "a public health emergency of international concern in January.

By March 11, The W.H.O. elevated the status to a pandemic. There were over 118,000 cases in 114 countries. Say waaaaat?!

In Jamaica we were still having events, still going to church, still going about our normal run of the mill days. And then it hit. It was not just close to home – it was home.

March 4, 2020 would have been a normal day for many. I was helping to plan a major event on Sunday, March 8 – The 10,000 Man March in Spanish Town. My friend, Markland "Action" Edwards, had buried his father the day before. We were there to show him support. My next event was Friday, March 13 at the Andrews High School for Girls. This is something I always look forward to…ministering at the various high schools…talking, singing, encouraging young people.

But it was not to be. You see on March 4 a Jamaican female who had travelled to the United Kingdom arrived in Jamaica. She went to the public health entity and was placed in isolation on March 9. She had the virus.

Let me encourage you that this chapter will get better…just as I believe God for all that we are seeing now. It will get better. I do recall as well leading worship on Sunday, March 8 and it was in my mind, singing over and over "Be Magnified Oh Lord" – Written by Lynn DeShazo. It was not fully clear until after why God placed that song in my heart. He wanted us to "MAGNIFY" His name over that of the virus. I sang like never before – I just wanted to exalt the name of Jehovah God as high as I could. I pray He was pleased.

Slowly, weekly and with careful planning, the Government of Jamaica began the daunting task of making announcements to keep the nation up to date. They then started to make hard decisions that would change our lives…maybe forever.

Church was no longer business as usual. We went from regular meetings to only having 20 persons together in one place. Then it changed again – we were down to a maximum of 10 persons in a setting.   If things became more unmanageable, the next announcement would see us moving to 5 and then to 2 and worst case would be all parties stay home indefinitely. It was like a scene from a movie.

There were memes, and comedy scenes – it changed how we did things. Meetings were now all on the internet. Church was now all social media and on traditional media (Radio and TV). It was not real…it could not be.

How could this be happening?

And then I heard it…Release "I Shall Live"
Release "I Shall Live"? When darkness, death and disaster was looming all over the world?

◆◆◆

I SHALL LIVE

Pastor Dean Smith is an anointed Man of God. I don't remember how we met, but I remember visiting his church some time ago and listening to him singing and worshipping. He is truly gifted.

I had shared in a service and sang the chorus for "That's Who You Are To Me – Way Maker" (see Chapter 1) and he was blessed by that. He felt led of The Lord to share a song with me and my group – how did he say it? He felt led to "sow a song in my ministry".

While listening to him in December 2015, I was searching for the songs he was singing and could not find them on the net. I asked his wife, where did he get the songs that he was singing…they were that good. She smiled and said that he had written them. Say what?!

I encouraged him later to record a few songs and get them registered immediately and begin registering his songs as they come live on stage. This gift is amazing.

I have such high respect for both Pastor Dean and Prophetess Sarah Smith. Pastor Dean wrote the song I talked about in Chapter 2 as well.

He was convinced that God wanted him to sow in my ministry and so the journey began. We set the time for studio and met for him to share the song with myself and my musicians.

Wednesday morning, I ran to the studio ready to hear what the song would be. Brinton Haughton, Karl Gibson, Wendell Lawrence, Pastor Dean and myself met. Jovan Norman came the next day and added guitar.

We prayed. And then he shared. He thought "Higher Place" was the song. But that morning – God gave him the song for us. I Shall not…I later changed the name to I Shall Live.

Here is what God gave Pastor Dean Smith to give to my ministry. Read the power in these words taken from scripture and think about the pestilence on the lands of the world now…Can you see why God would want us to release this song NOW?

I Shall Live – Written by Dean Smith

Verse One

The wicked surrounded me,
The plan of the enemy
Was to destroy my purpose, destroy my purpose
They came against me like bees,
But the sting of the wicked ceased
Cause Jehovah was with me to protect and to shield me
The Lord is my strength and He is my song
He has become my salvation
Whom shall I fear? Whom shall I fear?
The Lord is my light and through Him I fight
Everything will be alright
He is with me. He is with me

Chorus

I shall not
I shall not
I shall not die but live and declare His works
(Rept)

Verse Two

He covers me with His wings
I dwell in the secret place of the Lord God Almighty, the Lord
God Almighty
No terror will topple me,
His is strength is perfect in me
I am more than a conqueror,
More than a conqueror
One thousand will fall beside my left,
Even ten thousand at my right
But it won't come near me,
Jehovah Shammah is with me

> *No evil befall me, no plague will come near me*
> *He gives His angels charge over me, and they always keep*
> *me*
> *Encamping around me*

What a song! The deal was sealed and I am eternally blessed by this gift. As I heard it – release it now!!! I called my Producer, Wendell Lawrence and Musician, Rhon Mattison and we worked out how we would make it happen. Thank God Rhon already had the files – we donned him with the responsibility to balance, mix and master the song. Something he had very little experience with…he certainly had not mastered a song before.

These are technical, musical terms but all in all – it is what is done to a song to take it from bare so-so studio laying of instrument tracks and vocals and putting them together in a way that sounds pleasing to the ear.

And Rhon did a fantastic job.

But why release a song about Life now?

I wanted persons to speak life over their situations. The news was becoming more and more depressing and we just needed to be lifted. The song itself is a combination of various Psalms and includes Psalm 91 which was on so many person's tongues. Verse two is my favourite.

I have found myself driving around and thanking God for the opportunity to "right the wrongs". To come before His throne and cry – search me Oh God. To seek His face. To study His word. Jehovah God in His mercy gave us time.

Whether the rapture takes place in a day, one month, one year or 10 years from now…we have this time to speak life over our situations and to draw closer to God.

Don't be afraid of the news.
Don't stress about all that surrounds you.
Now is the time to sing to yourself
All the words from songs that have kept you.
Don't be stuck looking at the negative
The reality is rough, hard and cold
But somehow there is greater in all of this
Jehovah God's hands are there to hold.
Shut away with God in these moments
Lockdown with the Master of the Wind
Turn your eyes fully on Jesus
From all the sin you encouraged – rescind.
Don't be discouraged – It's look up time
Don't focus on the truths and the sad turns
Do remember God is STILL IN CONTROL
And Declare I SHALL LIVE AND DECLARE HIS WORKS.

Written by Nadine Blair
NADSINK

Know this…We have been given time. Value every second – every minute. Let God work in you. All the things that you need to correct do that now. I am scrambling to finish this book. To finish songs God has given me and truth be told – it should not have been so. I should have been on the beat and running in time with God.

See I too delay and wait. I too struggle with believing fully in things God has said do…and yes, I have been doing my "go to God again" trips and thank God for His mercy…He has extended to me Grace. Grace to make it right. Fortunately, God is more merciful than people.

We have been given this time to sing over our lives and the lives of our loved ones. Sing life and breathe life. Sing over your community. Sing over your country. Let not the news be your point of filling up. Let the Word of God be that point. It is important to be informed and be in the know of what is happening. But bigger than that is what is happening in the spirit.

I always say, what happens in the spirit world is more potent, more lasting, more concerning than what we see in the natural. So, Focus your eyes on the spirit.

Focus your eyes on the Word.

Focus your eyes on being ready for the rapture. Focus your eyes on your direct word from God – Go Live! Go do it! Go Sing Your Song.

And as you do…speak LIFE!

TICK TOCK

Woke up this morning and it was a brand-new year
The feeling of newness was so very clear
But this one was different
This one was not the same
This new year had double digits
And had us all singing again

Double for my trouble
A year of plenty oh
2020 Vision
And a bag of promises - more

This year some a guh married
We a get back what the enemy stole
This year there was something extra

To all those things we've heard before.

Woke up this morning
And I had a new attitude
My gym work out plan was in check
And so was my diet too

My plans are falling into place
Well at least the ones I focused on
Boy why every year must catch us
Failing at wi plan

Then came time for Lent
And I took on the challenge
Daniel Fast here I come
Well I will do what I can manage

Some days boy - I was just about To give up
and hang it all in
But this year I decided
21 days I must win

I watched as persons vacillated
Between pressing on and going through
And simply and easily giving up
On all the tasks and things to do

What dress to wear
What suit to don
What hair cut or style should I choose
The nails on flick
The shoes on flick
Look out world I'm coming through

Woke up this morning - Heard the news

of some outbreak far away
Oh no - bless their hearts - I'll pray for them
Jehovah please - make a away

Tick tock - goes the clock
Time - What will you reveal?
But wait - wasn't it just one little town
And now it's crossing borders - this can't be real

I'll pray for them...It's just so sad
Let me go back to life for me
What's my next event?
Oh a worship night - ah yes praise Jesus my King

But wait the plot thickens -
Why can't these people listen
Don't they hear the news over and ore
Tick Tock - goes the clock
Now souls are gone by the score

Woke up this morning and this thing jump over the sea
Come een like this virus a run after ....I won't say it No it
can't be
It move from far foreign to a place near to we
Tick Tock - goes the clock
Father How Could this be?

I remember the morning - the week before
I kept hearing "Sing Be Magnified"
So early Sunday morning March 8 to be exact
This was a part of my worship - a part of my cry

And then I heard it loud and clear
Jehovah God wanted us to Big Him up
Exalt Him - Lift Him High with our praise

Magnifiy Him - we just could not stop

That was the sunday and all was set
For the next event I had to check
I was going to a school to chill with some youths
And lead some soul to Christ with the Truth

Tick Tock Goes the Clock
Thick Thick gets the plot

Woke up one morning and everything changed
Events were cancelled
No one was calling my name
That thing that start twenty-leventeen miles away
Had somehow reached our borders
Someone make it go away

Since that day
That dark dark day
Church door lock
And mi good-up hair and nails took a vacay

Now I don't bother to worry about the dress and the heels
In fact a so so flats me a wear - and masks - my make up
less face to conceal

Woke up one morning and in the midst of the seize
I found myself thankful for some unobvious things
God actually mek wi stop - right braps in a wi space
Fi check wiself - To introspect - To upon His presence gaze

Tell you no lie - I wonder when will ever go
Back to what we knew as normal
Or will we surrender to this new and forget
What we knew as formal

The biggest thing for me now is - is my heart right with God
Have I done all He wants me to - nah lie - a dat me deh pon

For if He comes today or tomorrow - or the next ten years
from now
Our position must always be
To live or die is Christ all out

Woke up this morning - nothing else mattered
Can't hug no one anymore
Wonder how many persons I could have
Hugged, loved or forgave
All the things we could have done before we woke up...that
morning

Tick Tock Goes the Clock

Eternity waits Now that's the real stock
When after all of this - after all is said and done
There is more on the other side of waking up to conundrums

For one day we will dream our last dream
And begin to live with Christ for eternity
But let us in this moment STOP
Before the last tick of the Eternity Clock
...
And ensure that our souls are ready
Covid can't take us from that ultimate journey
So hold on tight - during this abnormal storm
Until we will wake up ...to eternal morns
Tick Tock...Tick Tock...Tick

Written by NADSINK
Nadine Blair - April 21, 2020 - 7am

Chapter 11
SING YOUR SONG – What's the Worst That Could Happen?

Take the name of Jesus with you... Take Him at His word. Trust Him and watch it come to pass.

I don't think I am the only one who has crazy faith for others and when it comes to me, I feel like I have to be cranked up and oiled to fiercely believe. We can get so easily discouraged by the words of people – often times people who are themselves struggling with something. Sometimes it is something they don't even realize or have come to own.

I love the Word of God in 2 Peter 1:3 King James Version (KJV) I mentioned it earlier.

"According as his divine power hath given unto us all things that pertain unto life and godliness, through the knowledge of him that hath called us to glory and virtue"

Everything we need to live a Godly life is given to us. But we have to KNOW Him. Yes, by the "Knowledge of Him". So, let us come to the table – casting fears aside. Come to the table leaving worries and our feelings of "less than" behind.

Let us come to God ready to be used. Revelation will come when we spend time in His Word – in His presence.

Look back at your life now. Stop. And Think. Really think about your life. Have you given your best? Have you done the best you could, in all you could, because you could? Sometimes I wish I had all the support I needed to get all the many tasks I have to do done... to get all the dreams and ideas I have in my mind – done. But I have to take the blame for simply not believing enough.

If I had one dollar for every idea that has come to my mind to do and I let unbelief and lack of support drown them out or put a delay on them until it just died, I'd be a rich woman today. Many times, I end up seeing the same dream or idea being done by someone else. And that kills me inside. Because I know it was a God-move that I just sat there and allowed the negative to silence me. I will have to answer to God for all those times. Don't let this be your story.

If God has given you an idea, JUST START. Don't wait on the perfect moment. Start. Pray over it and ask God for all you need to make it happen.

If He showed it to you, it is for a purpose. And often that purpose is not really all about you... but ultimately for souls and the glory of His Kingdom. If God allowed you to see something in the spirit – it can be that you are seeing something that will happen and you are a part of the prayer team He has assigned to pray it through.

I remember years ago I was driving by the crossing of Spanish Town Road and Hagley Park Road. As I drove, I saw roads on top of roads. I said to myself, that it would be awesome to see in the natural what I was seeing in my mind's eye. Well, those of us in Jamaica now are seeing it – for real. It's almost like pudding – (big laugh) – one road at the bottom and two overlapping highways *a top*... we now have three roads on three different levels in that intersection.

Did God want me to make the roads? I doubt that. But He allowed me to see something that would happen. Something I could pray about... oh that I did though. Understanding is something we should all pray for. Colossians 1:9 says it nicely, "that ye might be filled with the knowledge of his will in all wisdom and spiritual understanding..." (KJV).

Take this for every single thing that you do. Let it be your prayer. And yes, this became another song as I prayed one day. I wanted so much to ensure I remembered this beautiful verse that I asked the Lord for a little tune... and it flowed... without changing much.

Let me be filled with the knowledge of Your will;
With all wisdom and understanding of
spiritual things

Written by Nadine Blair
Inspired by Colossians 1:9

A simple chorus that I pray to develop and sing for the world – so others may remember this powerful prayer in scripture – Colossians 1:9.

We need the wisdom to understand when it is something for us to do and when it is something for us to pray through. Either way, prayer must be a part of it, but God may allow you to see something happening that is not necessarily for you to do but for you to commit to prayer.

This is crucial to learn to differentiate. It can also be something for you to pass on to someone else to do. But woe of woes if it was something for you to do and He got tired of waiting on you to believe. I believe God has gotten tired of waiting on me several times. But His Grace won't give up on me and for this I am grateful. Feel bad – naaa lie. So why do I write now? Because I must. I have so much in me and I cannot wait any longer.

What is it that you have in you? What dream? Desire? Plan? I pray your faith will be stirred to a new level.

Don't think about it... just dive in and do it. The more you think about it is the more you will find one million excuses why it should not be done – *yet*. And the time you take to wait for the perfect time, someone else will get up and do it.

A friend shared a story of a vision she had, to do something in her community. She waited and waited and then braps! – someone else started to do it. Well she talked with her pastor and upon advice she really believed that even though someone else started it, there was still room for her to do her thing. She started it and ran it for a few years. Many people were blessed by her business – a school – a training ground for many to learn more about God.

Lord, give us the wisdom to discern when to run with it or give it up. You see, sometimes when someone else has started something similar you need to move on. But there are times when even when someone else has started a similar move, it doesn't mean that you can't still do what was in your belly. It may now look like you are following a trend, but do it anyway. Pray about it. Keep your heart pure. And do it.

What do I mean by "keep your heart pure" – well that ground can easily become a "watch how I can do this better than you" ground if you are not careful. "Keep your heart pure" means do it with no ill thought towards the other person who is doing that similar thing. Of course, now you will have to tweak it and make it a little different but do it anyways... but when you do...

Keep your heart pure
Let your motives be Godly
He will fill you with His knowledge
Wisdom and spiritual understanding

Let prayer be your foundation
The Holy Spirit your guide
Jesus your pilot
And Jehovah God will abide.

Written by Nadine Blair
NADSINK

As you walk this road, remember the coming of our Lord is near. Your assignment is tied to you still breathing. You are still on this earth for purpose to be fulfilled. We all won't have the same platform and tasks but we must – each of us – do the bidding of our Father.

In John Bunyan's classic book *Pilgrim's Progress*, we see a beautiful description of the lead actor, "Christian" and how he faces challenges day in day out. We are privy to the many choices he has to make and the resultant consequences of bad choices – even when his intention was good.

The wonderful grace of our Lord Jesus goes beyond our hiccups and failures. But let us never think that we should take God's grace for granted.

Don't just lean back and say He will forgive. His grace does not give us license to keep on disobeying Him. "Nuh tek God fi poppy show" (Don't approach God as if He's a pushover or pretender.)

Be diligent to serve.
Be dedicated in purpose.
Be decisive in action.
Be dauntless in your pursuit.
With God in the midst...what's the worst that can happen?

BRAWTA

EXCERPT FROM MY NEXT BOOK…

"NADINE BLAIR – The Woman, The Worshipper, The Witness"

1

One Door Closes, Another One Opens

My life as a PK (Pastor's Kid) brought with it numerous opportunities and yet many challenges. My three sisters and I had to walk a tightrope as our lives were not our own but belonged to the prying eyes of the congregants. Well, that's how it felt. As the saying goes, "if we slip, we slide". I remember one Sunday morning how my sister Delva poured out her feelings on the microphone. She just wanted to be allowed to grow up – make the mistakes and learn from them. Well, I'm not sure if it worked but some persons got a feeling that this PK thing though filled with limited glamour had its downside.

There were also times when because you were the PK you "get a blie" so you got to skip the line, favour extended to you, and so on. And that had its pros and cons. What it did for me then, was give me a sense that I could get anything I wanted. So if we weren't careful we could easily grow up as spoilt brats.

Our parents, however, brought the balance. We had to remain "normal kids" – so we cleaned, cooked, washed, answered properly, and showed respect to elders. Or you can be sure that a whooping would be ours if we thus strayed.

There were times when Dad would be at the podium and correct us from up there. It was all good and helped to keep the balance. But why didn't the so-called favour not translate in other areas of our lives?

I attended Immaculate Conception High School and I remember for years wondering why I was never chosen to receive the "Good Citizenship Award". I remember sitting year after year and Sister Maureen Clare Hall (I so love this woman) would call name after name, class after class – and my name was never called. I was a good student. I made friends. I helped others. "And besides, I'm a PK!!!" But no, not one year was I considered for this award – not until my fourth or was it fifth year. Wow.

You can't imagine the shock when I heard my name. Ha... joy unspeakable. I had to learn through those years of waiting, that even though my name was not called for the "Good Citizenship Award", I had to maintain a high standard of character. I had to choose to not let the negative thoughts take over me.

Let us glory in this – "...*that our names are written in heaven.*" Paraphrased from Luke 10:20 KJV

My dad was now the Overseer for our denomination, The New Testament Church of God – known worldwide as The Church of God with international offices in Cleveland, Tennessee. With this – the opportunity was ours as children to study overseas – on scholarships, of course! But there was a *but*... we had to be 21 years or younger.

Me being the eldest and already 21, we thought this was just not going to happen for me so my sister, Delva, was shipped off and was enjoying her first year at Lee College... now Lee

University.

I applied to attend C.A.S.T – College of Arts, Science and Technology – now UTech – University of Technology. It was going to be perfect. I would give up working and go full-time to study whatever it was that was in my heart at the time. And me being me – of course I would be accepted. "After all, I'm a Pastor's Kid – right?!"

WRONG!!!

My heart skipped a couple beats when the letter came. This was going to be the continuation of a journey that I was on to further my studies. So we opened and started to read.

What do you mean *unfortunately*? Seriously? Really? For real? No, this just can't be happening. They denied me entry.

You can't imagine the feeling of devastation that hit me. "What am I supposed to do now? They really rejected me. Me? But I got the Good Citizenship award." Maybe it was a mistake. So many thoughts were running through my head. And all I wanted to do was walk.

So, I set out to walk. Where I was going? Only God knows. I remember mom was sitting on the verandah and as I stepped past her, she asked, "Where are you going?" I don't remember what I said but I remember the feeling... I just wanted to walk. It was just too much.

And then Mom said the magic words. "Nadine – one door close... another one open" in typical Jamaican fashion.

More anon...

About The Author

Nadine Annetta Blair

Anointed, Articulate and Charismatic are some adjectives that best describe *Nadine Annetta Blair*.

Born in Hanover, Jamaica on September 21, Nadine is the first of four children to Bishop Dr Ronald & Rev Evon Blair. Nadine rose to prominence in Jamaica when she was employed as a Host at Love FM at its inception in 1993. She quickly became the darling of gospel radio and maintained that position throughout the years which has resulted in her receiving the MAJA Awards for Media Personality in Gospel for 2006.

"Aunty Nadine", as she was affectionately called by 'her children' when she hosted Love FM's Kiddies Corner for many years, has a passion for Worship and Prayer. She is the Founder and CEO of Allowed to Shine Ministries (ATSM) which oversees:

- "Perpetual Praise", a 3-hour Worship and Praise session done in churches, schools, communities all across Jamaica, the Caribbean and internationally which started in 2002 (Now Called *Perpetual Sounds of Praise*);

- "Singled Out", Conferences dealing with issues affecting both single men and women which started in 2006;

- "When the Ministers Meet To Pray", Gospel Artistes, Ministers etc. meet to pray together which began in January of 2007 and evolved into the more official *Jamaica Gospel Music Network - JGMN* (now on pause)

- Praise in da Streets, a strategic move which started with Praise Partners - Chosen Vessel - to go into each parish capital with Praise and worship with a focus on spiritual warfare geared towards uniting the Churches and community to take back Jamaica under God.

Nadine holds a Bachelor of Arts Degree in Mass Communications from Lee University in Cleveland, Tennessee and was listed among *"Who's Who among Students"*. She currently hosts "Morning Express" aired on Love 101 FM – 10am to 1pm - Mondays to Fridays and also "Love In The Morning" on Fridays 5am to 10am. She also holds the position of Programmes Manager. Nadine is a well sought after Emcee for many local and international events including:

∂ Glory Music productions including - Fun in the Son (since its inception)
∂ Co-Emcee with The Bobby Jones at Event Montego Bay, Jamaica
∂ Introduced Gospel DJ Papa San at one of the events held at Gospel Music Week (the premiere Gospel event held before the Gospel Music/Dove Awards - the Gospel equivalent to the Grammy's, held in Nashville, Tennessee, USA)
∂ Life Production Concerts
∂ Honeycomb Gospel Awards

∂ JCDC Gospel shows and finals (Jamaica Cultural Development Commission)

∂ Henry Fernandez Faith Convention, Jamaica

∂ New Testament All Island Youth Congress

∂ Concerts featuring Artistes including Michael W. Smith, Mary Mary, Sandy Patti, Fred Hammond, Yolanda Adams, Kirk Franklin and Donnie McClurkin and others

Nadine is an enthusiastic Christian and is a member of the New Testament Church of God.

She is a Board Member of Jamaica Youth For Christ; she was the President of the Board of JGMN and also served her alma mater - Lee University as a Board Member for four years.

"I want to effect change in people's lives through my ministries and if that is accomplished then I would have fulfilled what God has purposed me to do," she pronounced.   The motto for her Allowed To Shine Ministries aptly summarizes Nadine's sentiment..,

**"Christ through us
To Others,
For Others to Shine".**

**Facebook - @nadineblairjamaica
* Twitter - @NadineABlair
* Instagram - @NadineBlairJA
* YouTube – Nadine Blair
Website –** *http://perpetualsoundsofpraise.com*
Donations – *https://www.paypal.me/NadineBlairJA*